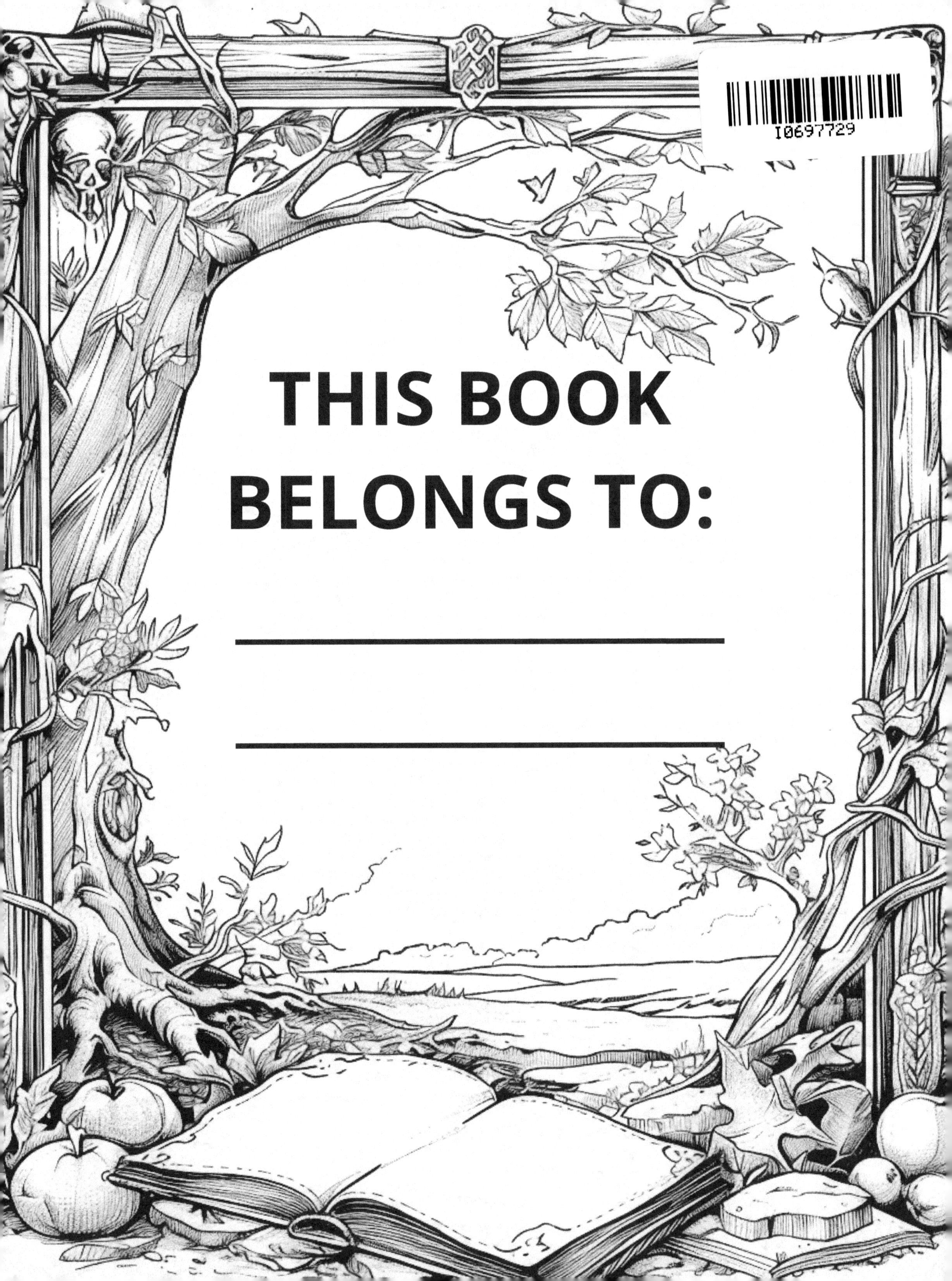
I0697729
THIS BOOK
BELONGS TO:

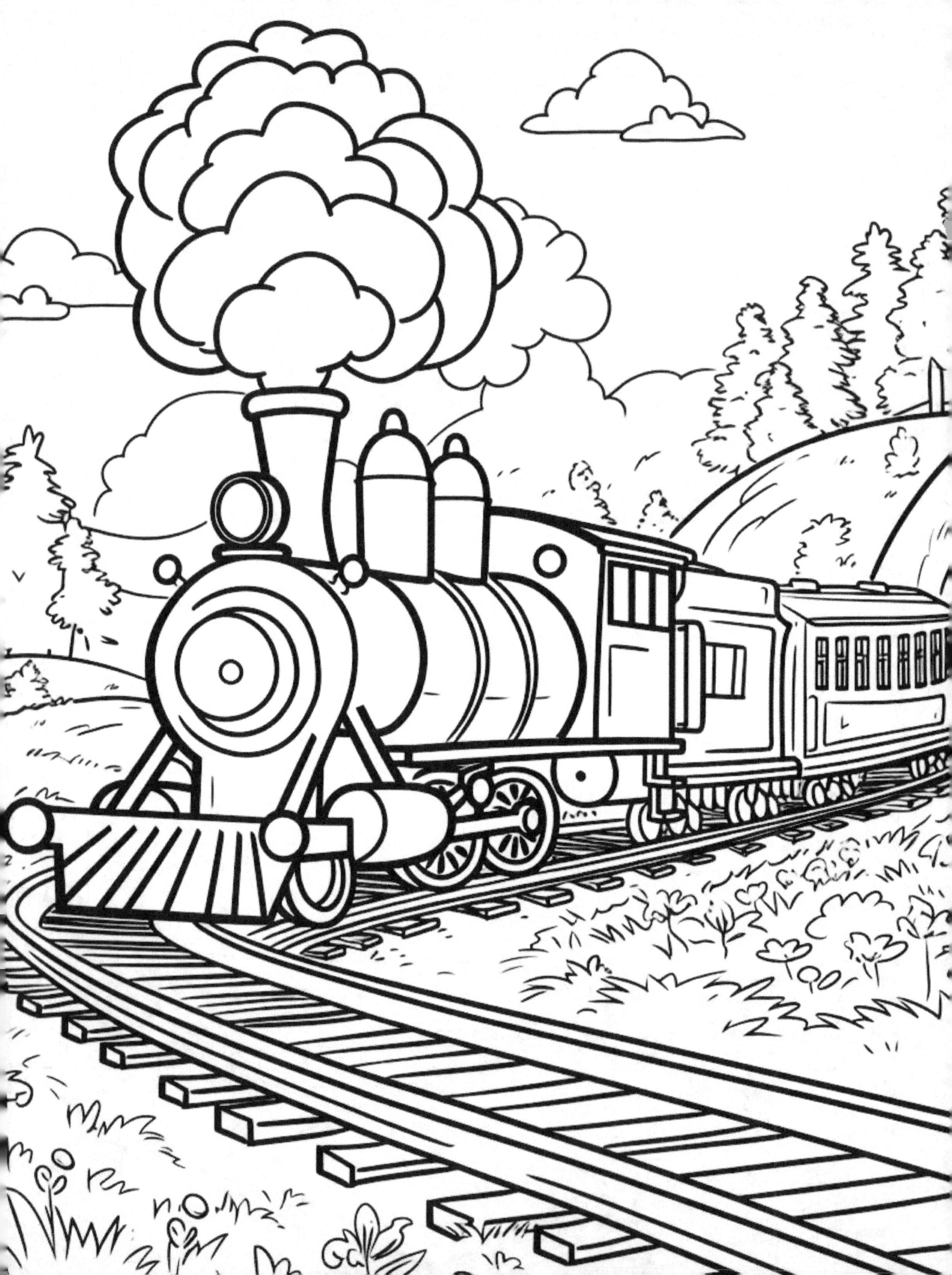

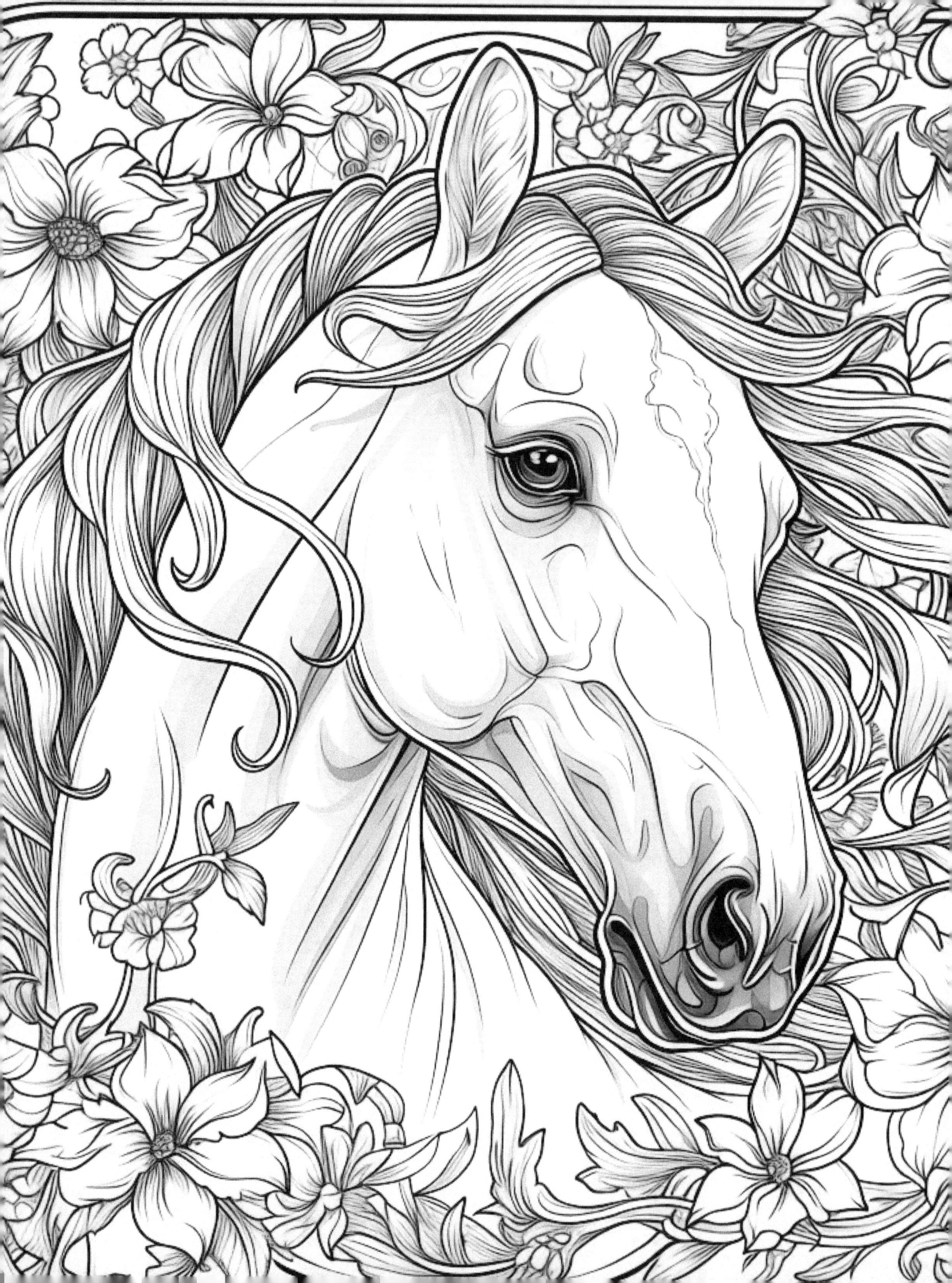

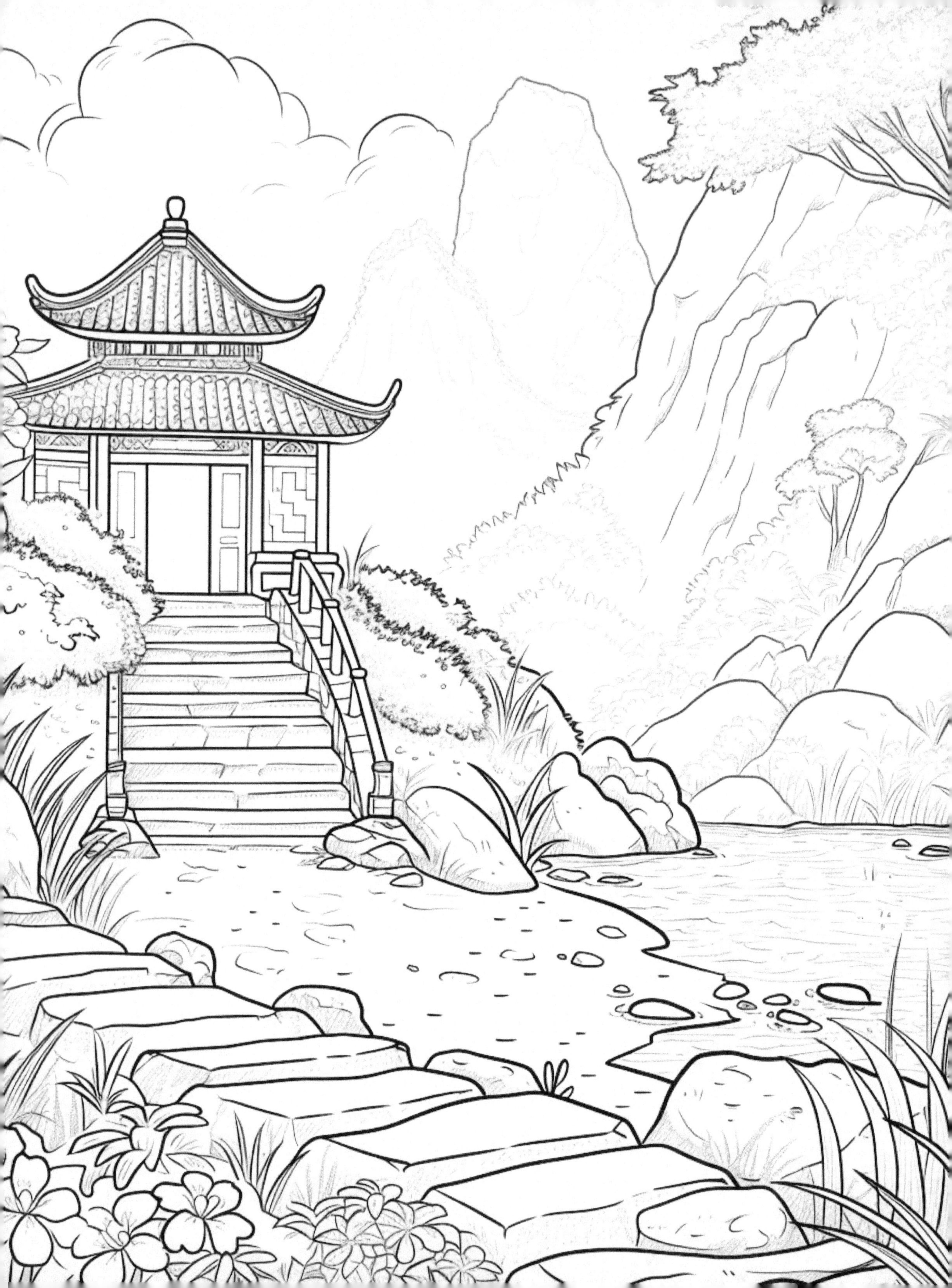

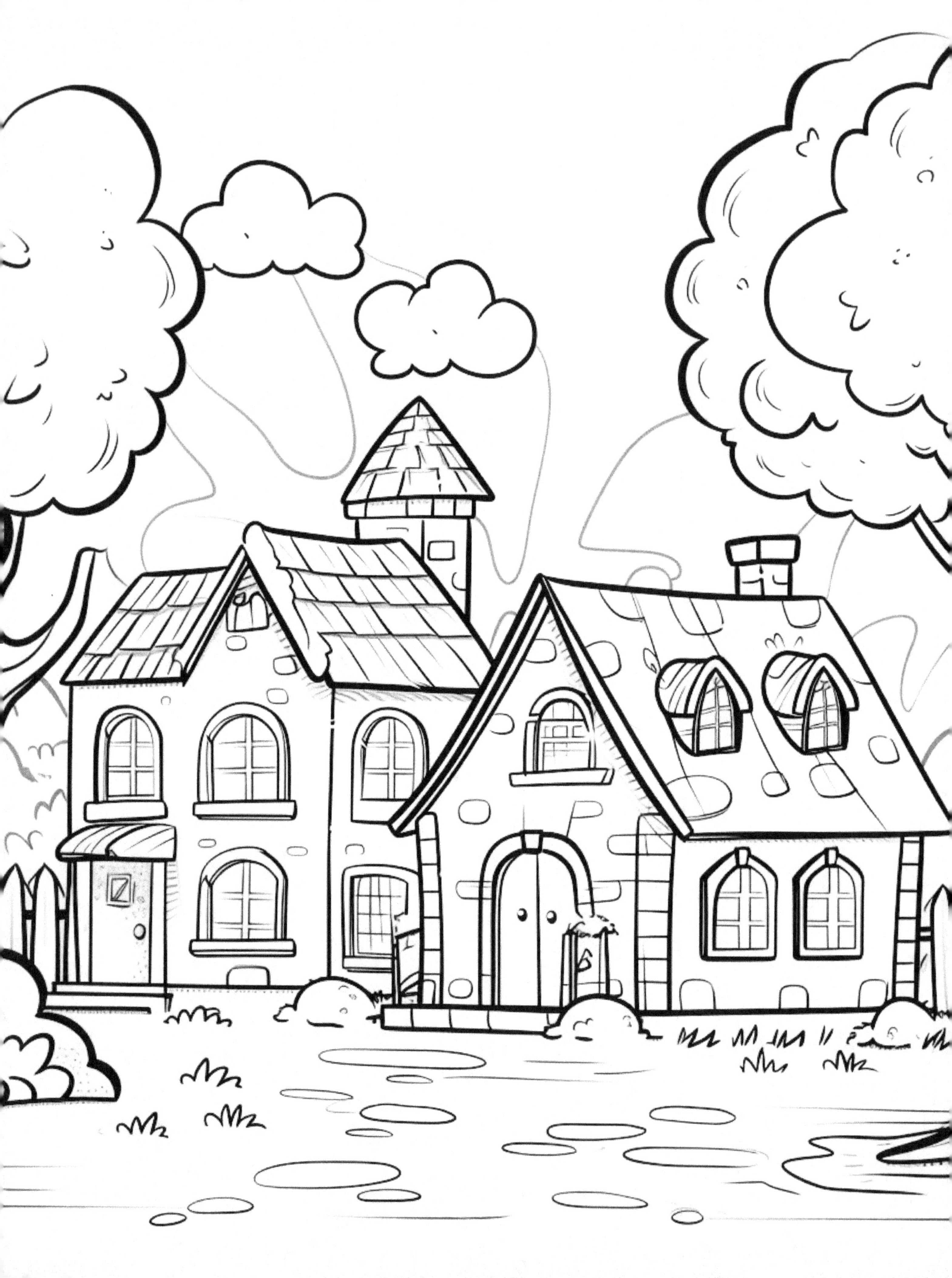

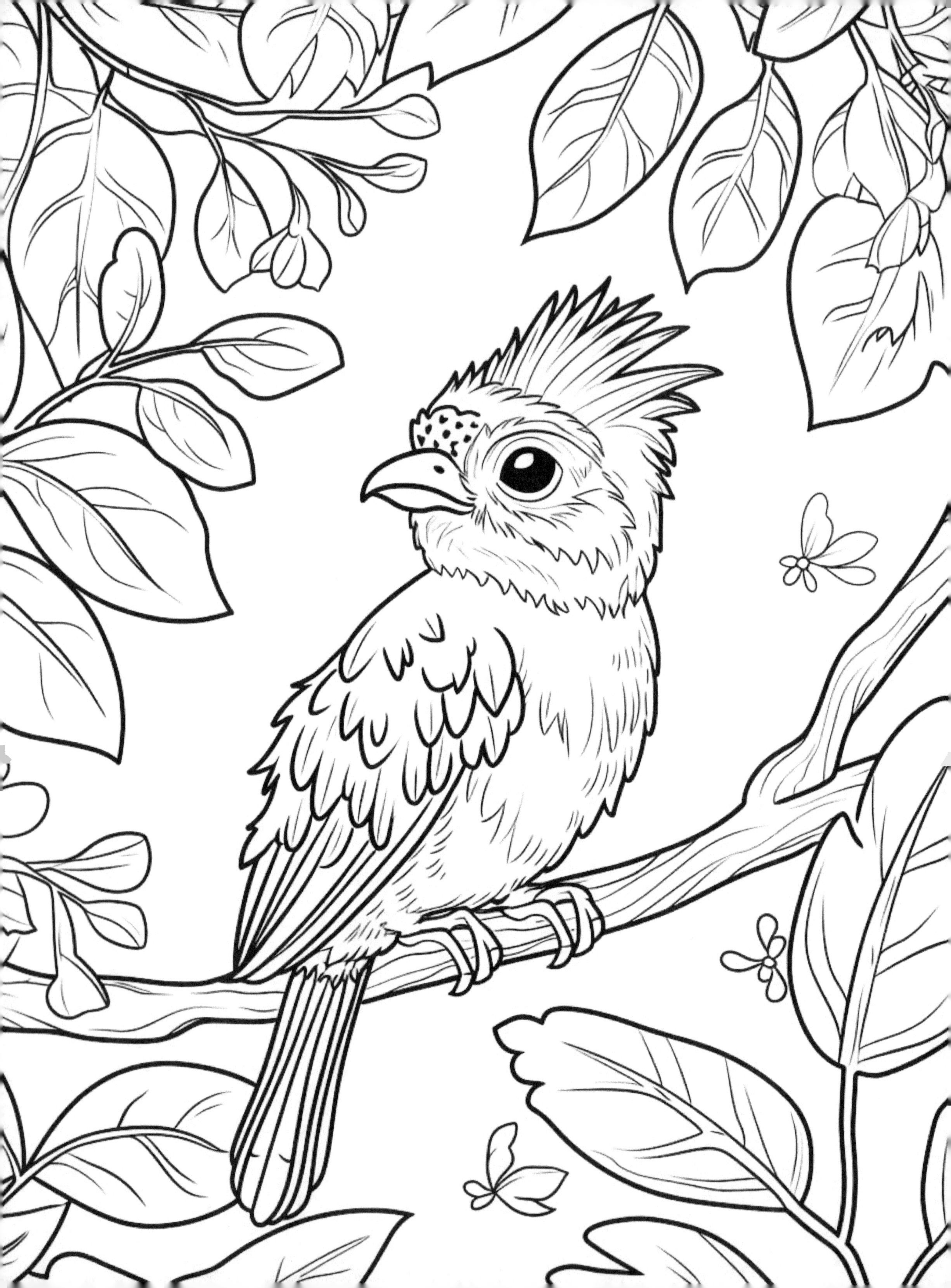

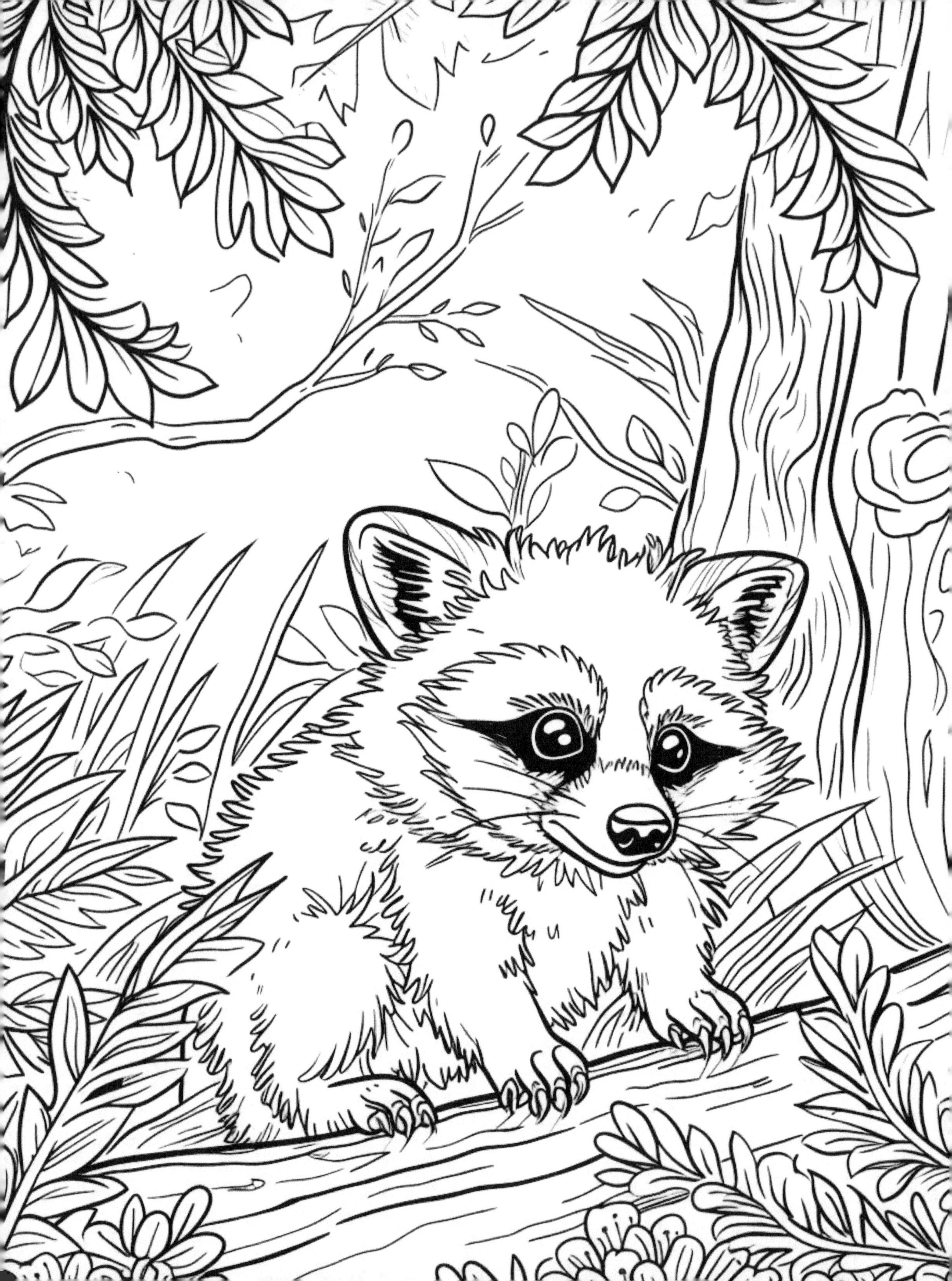

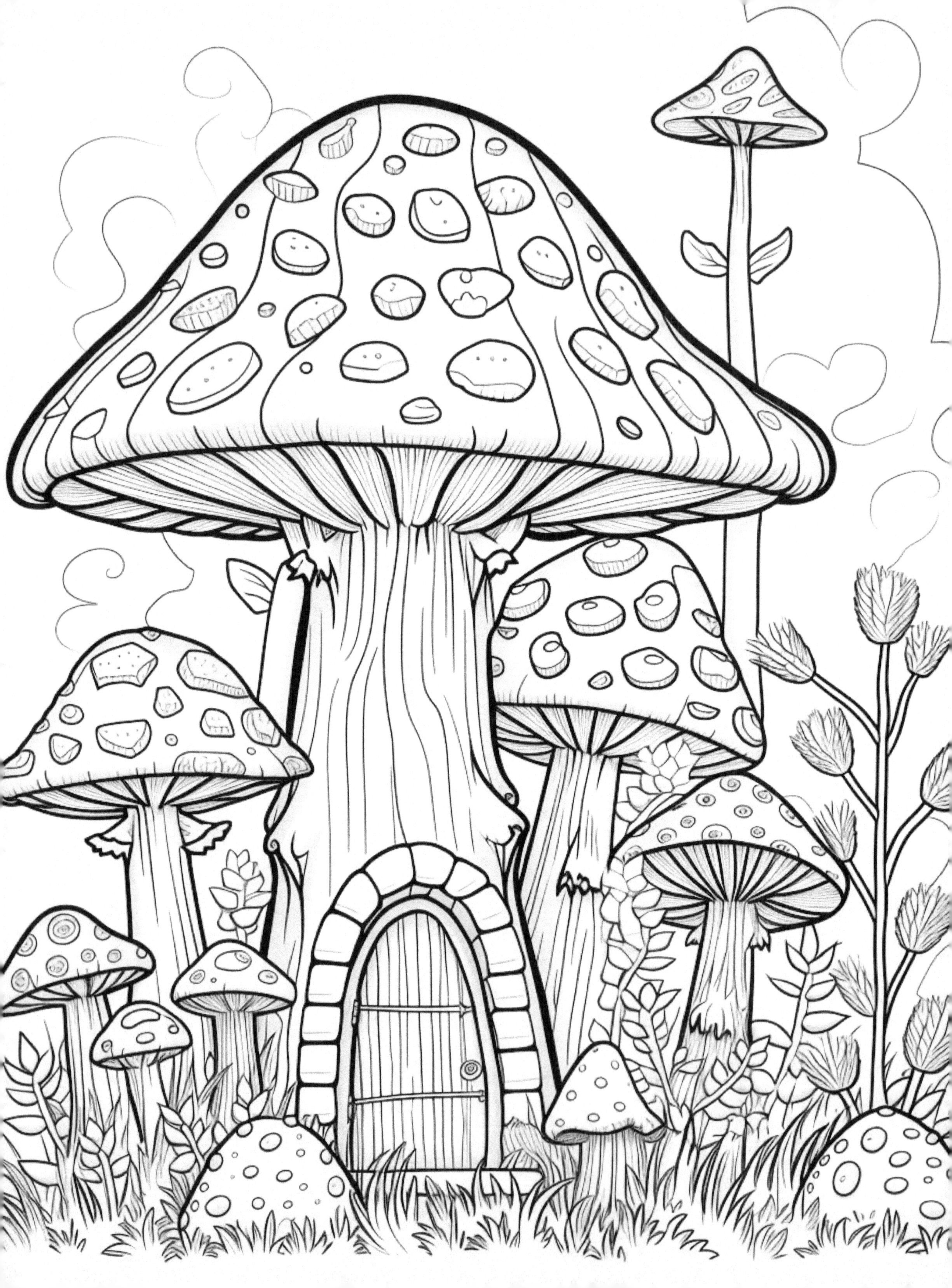

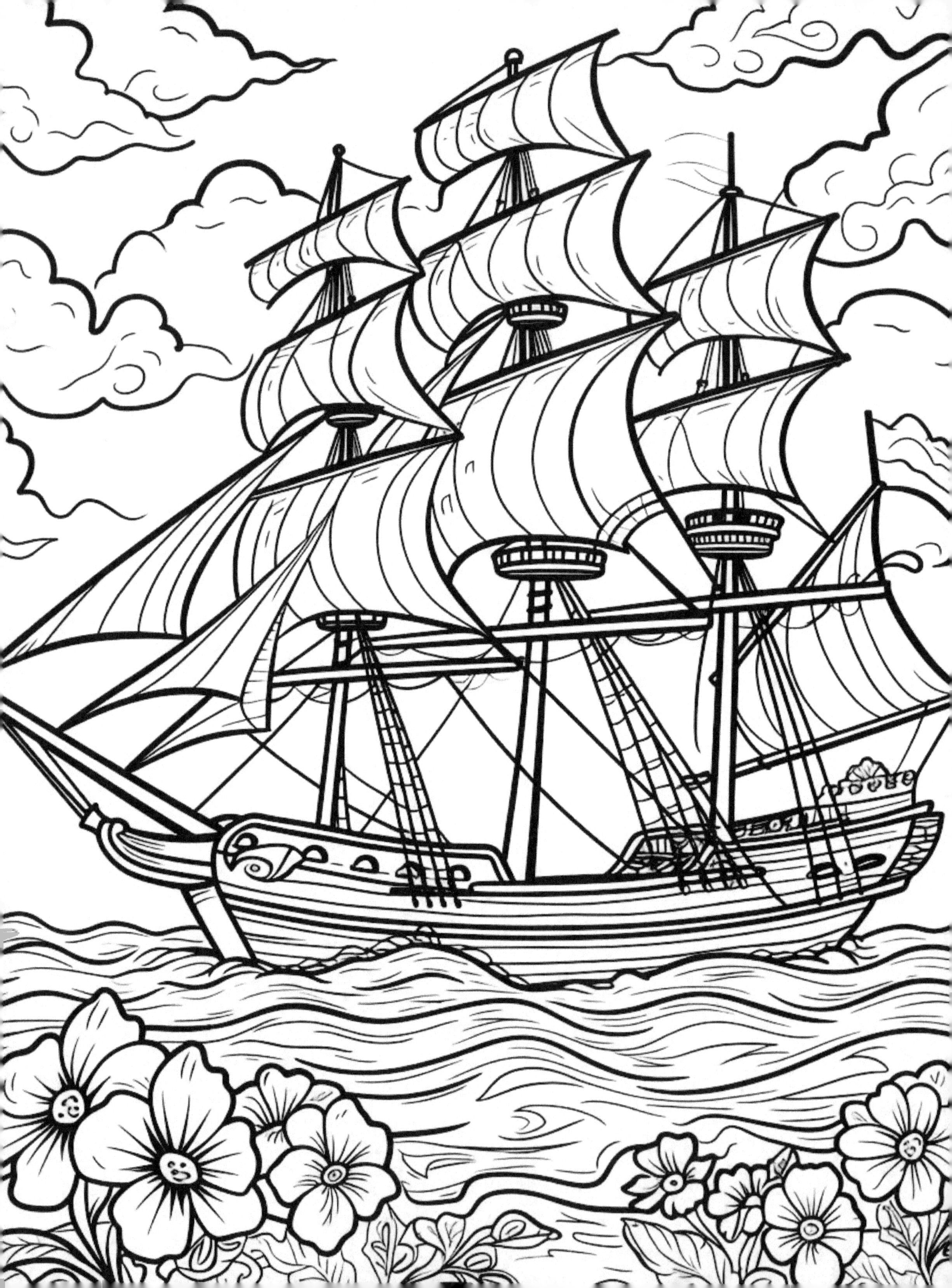

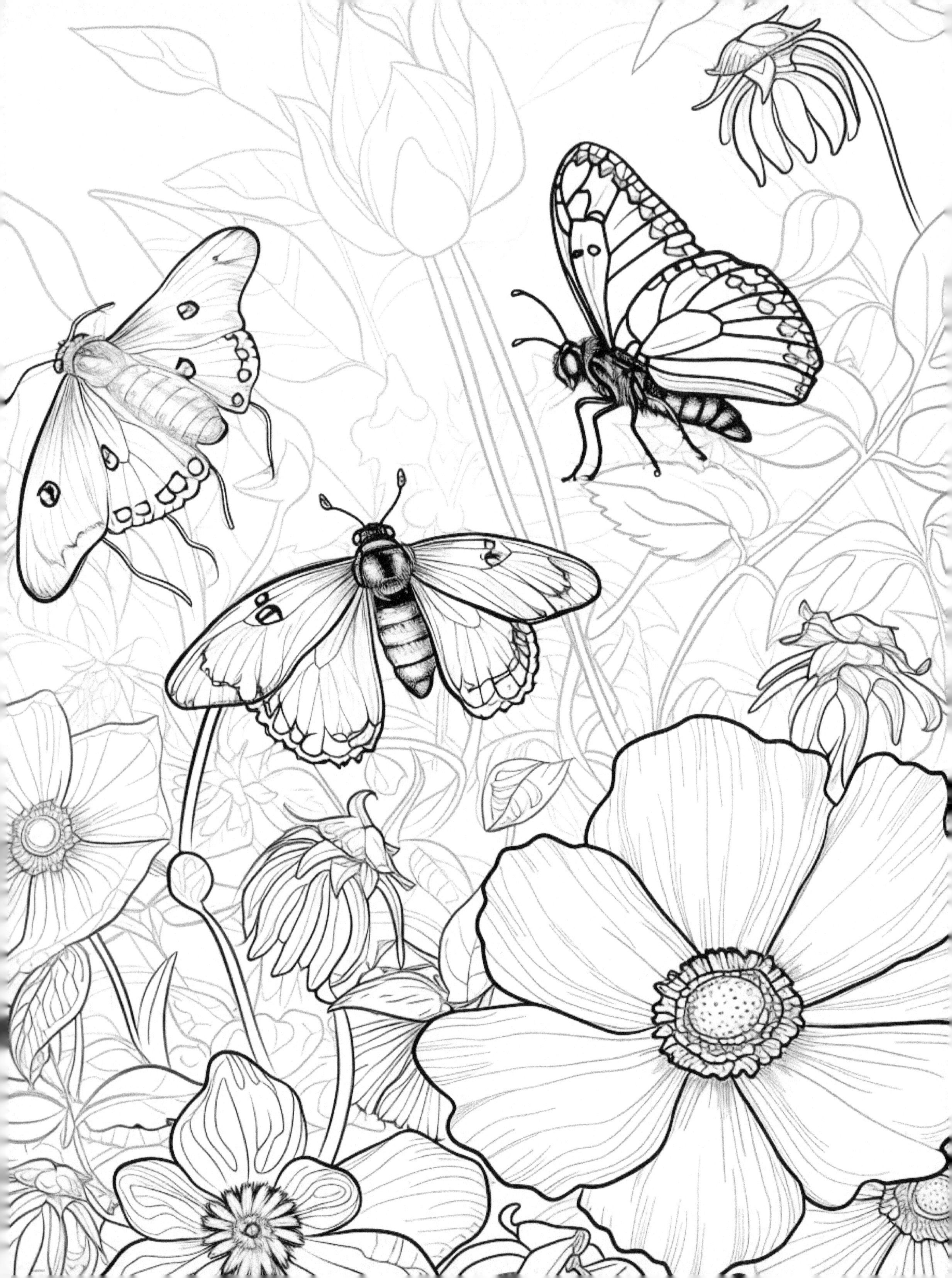

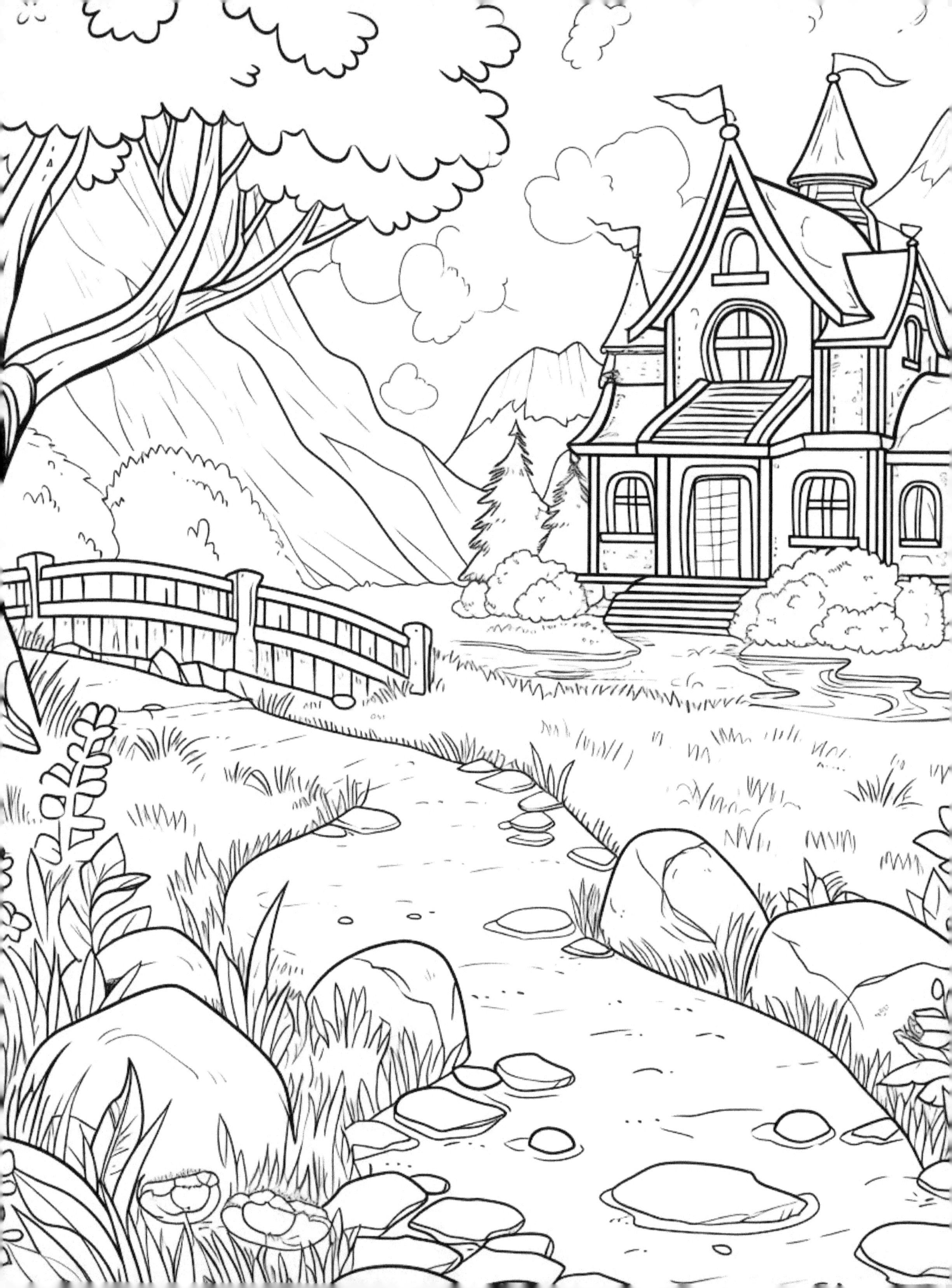

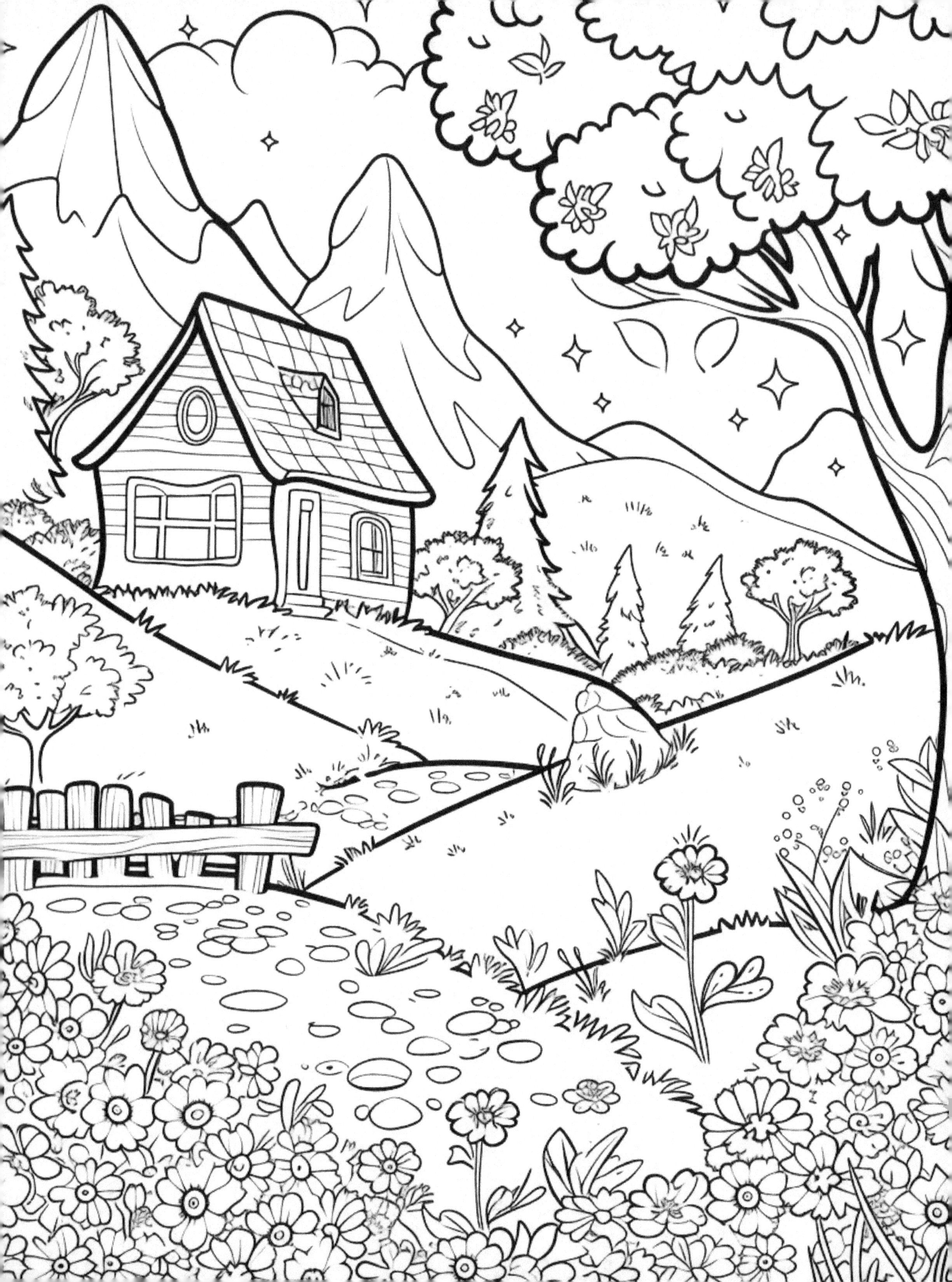

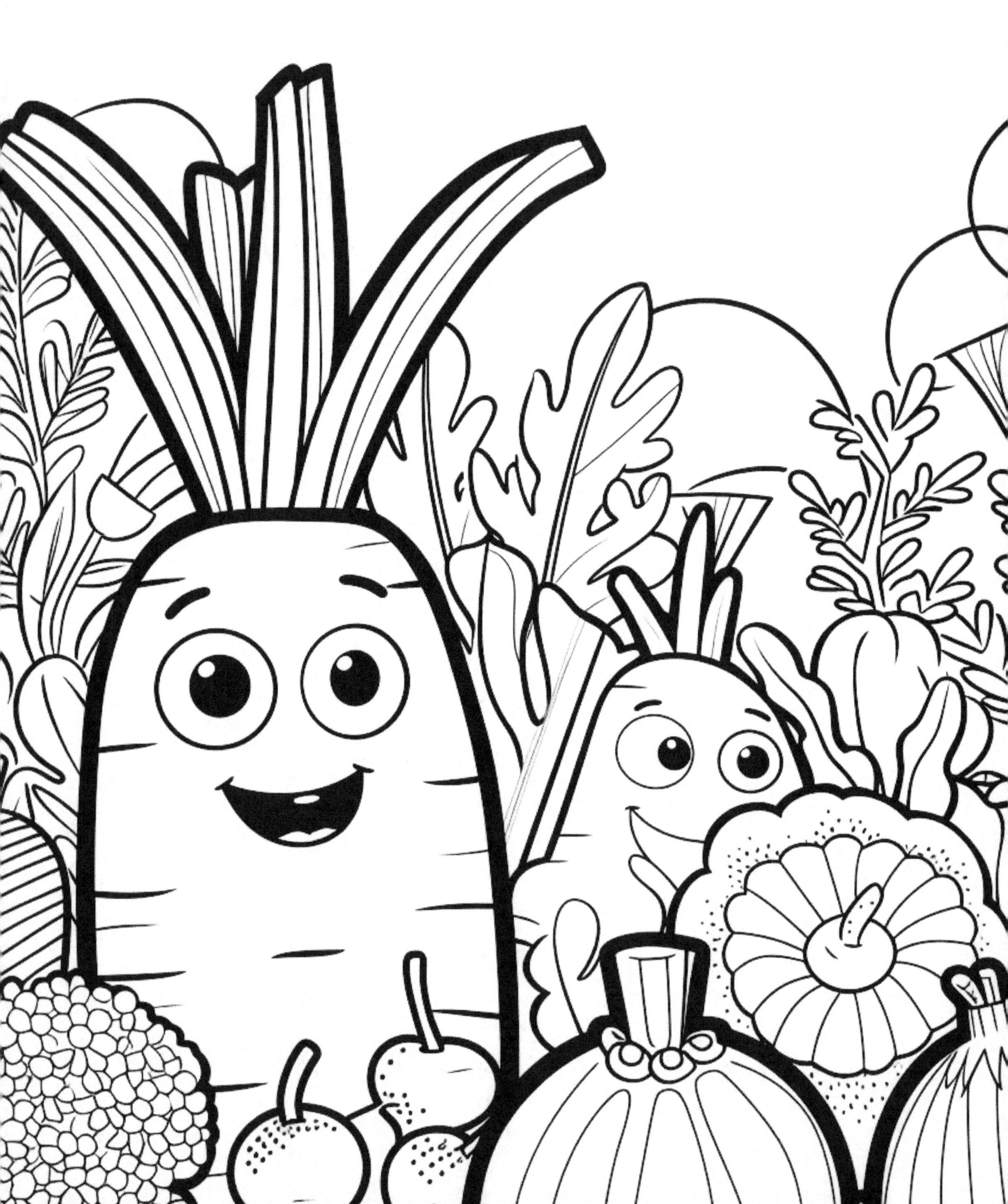

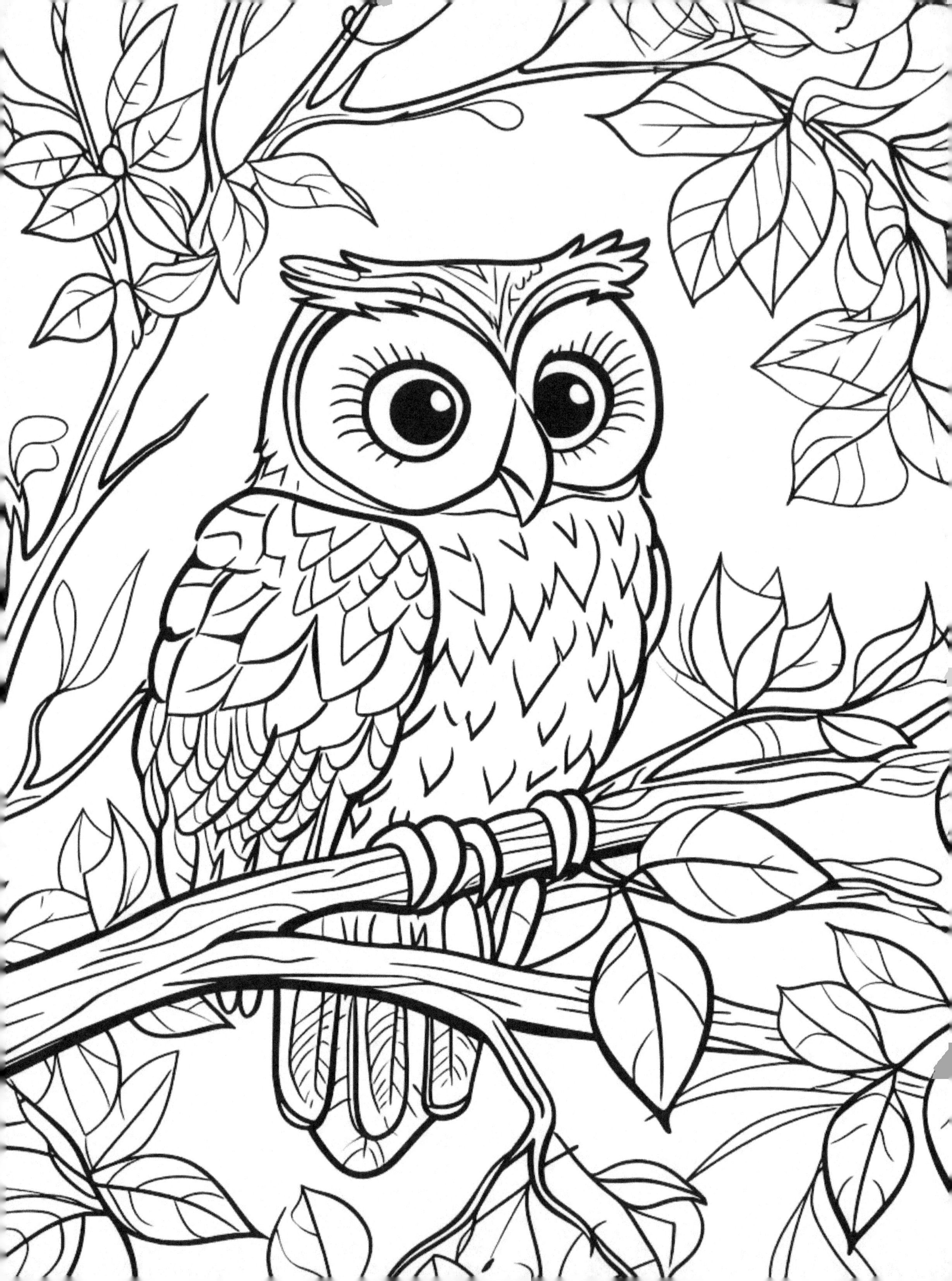

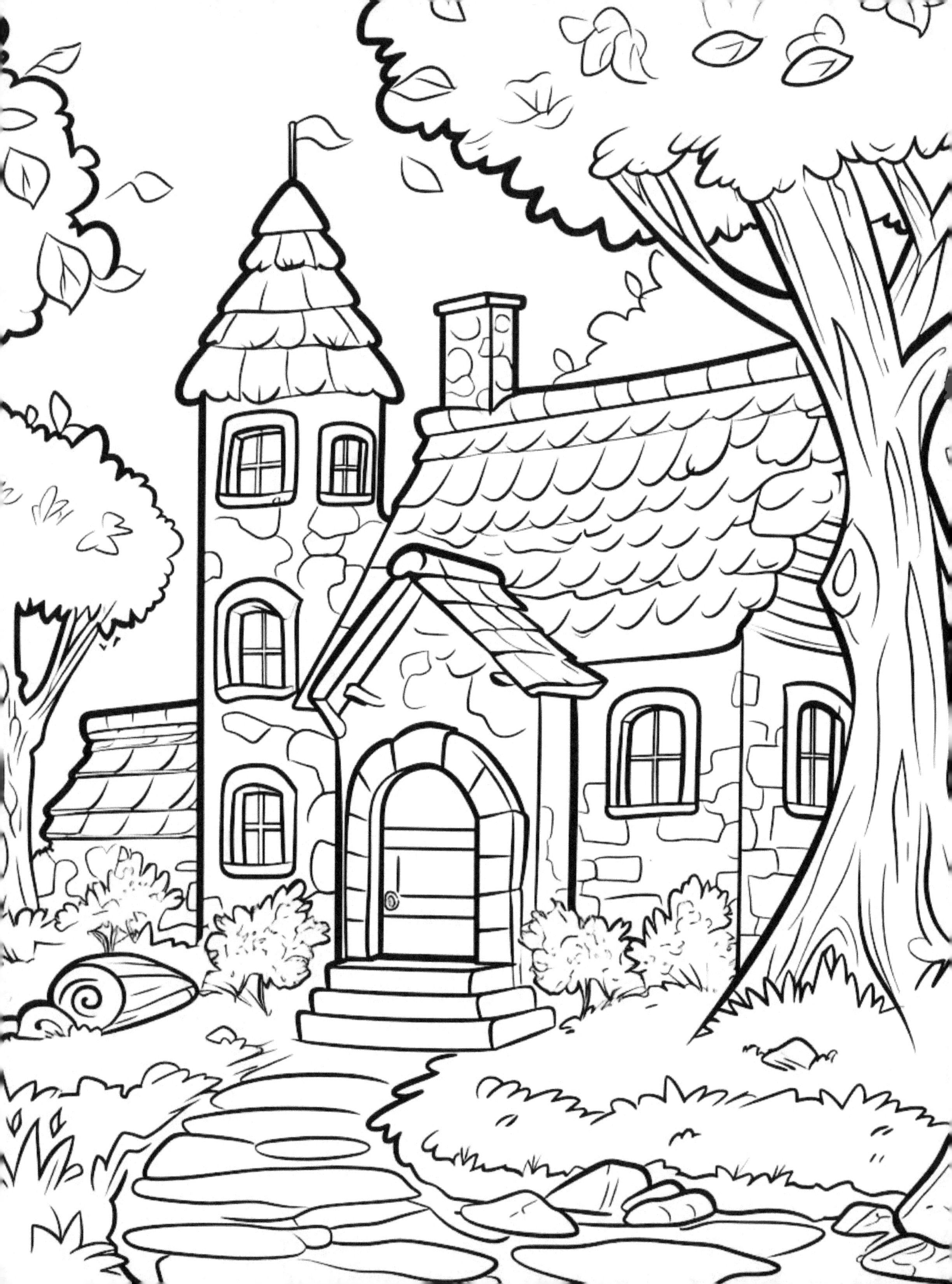

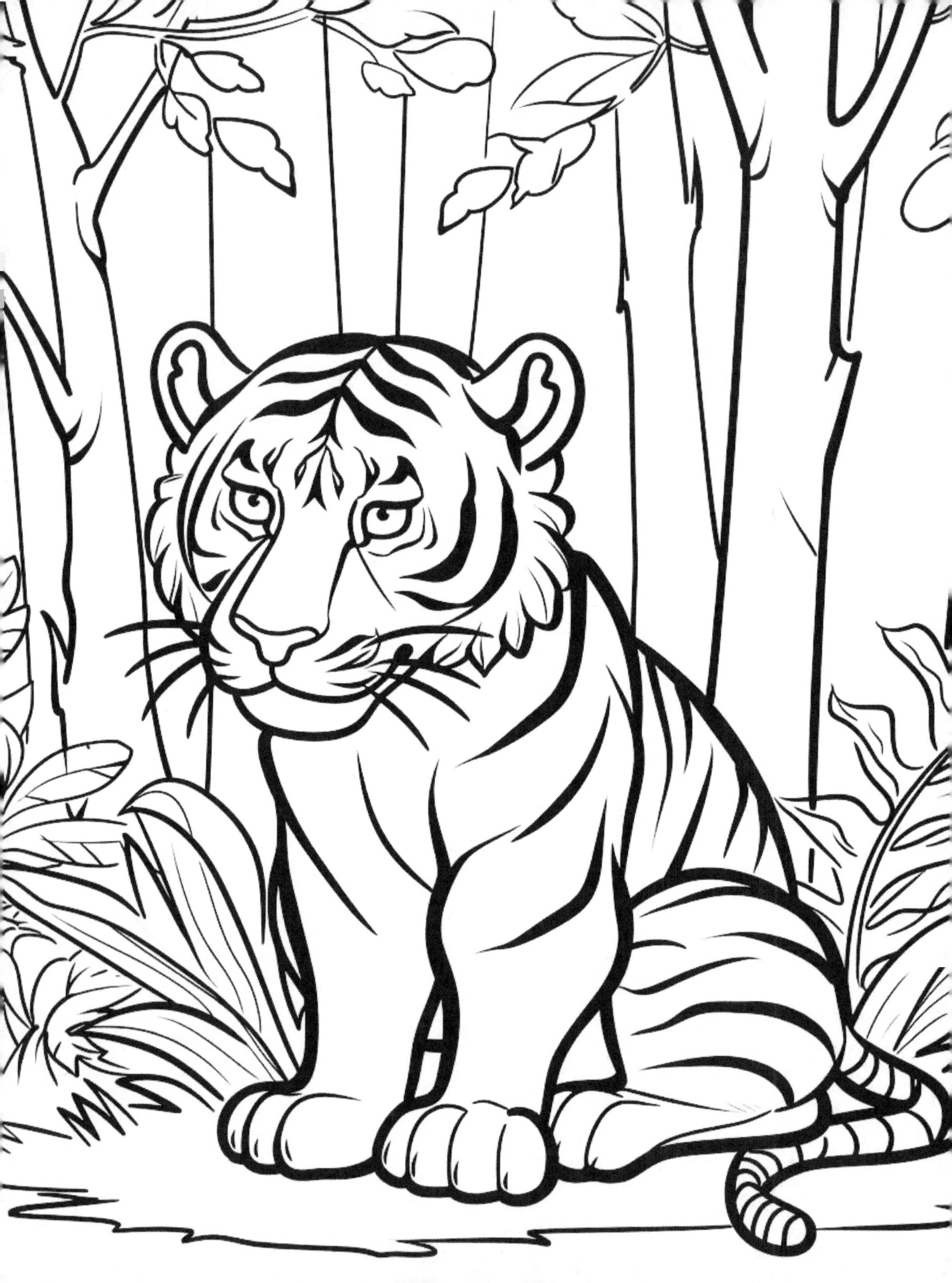

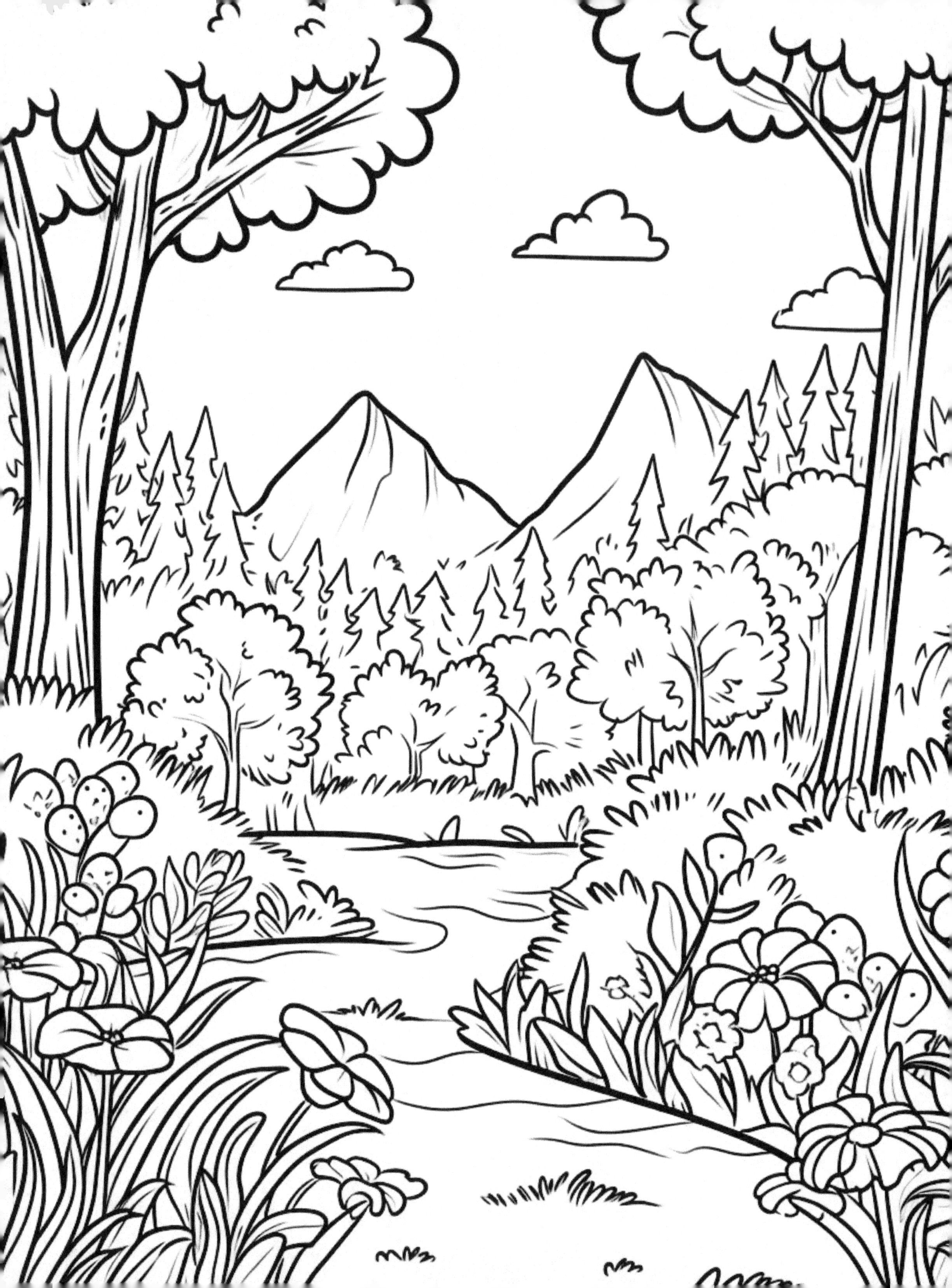

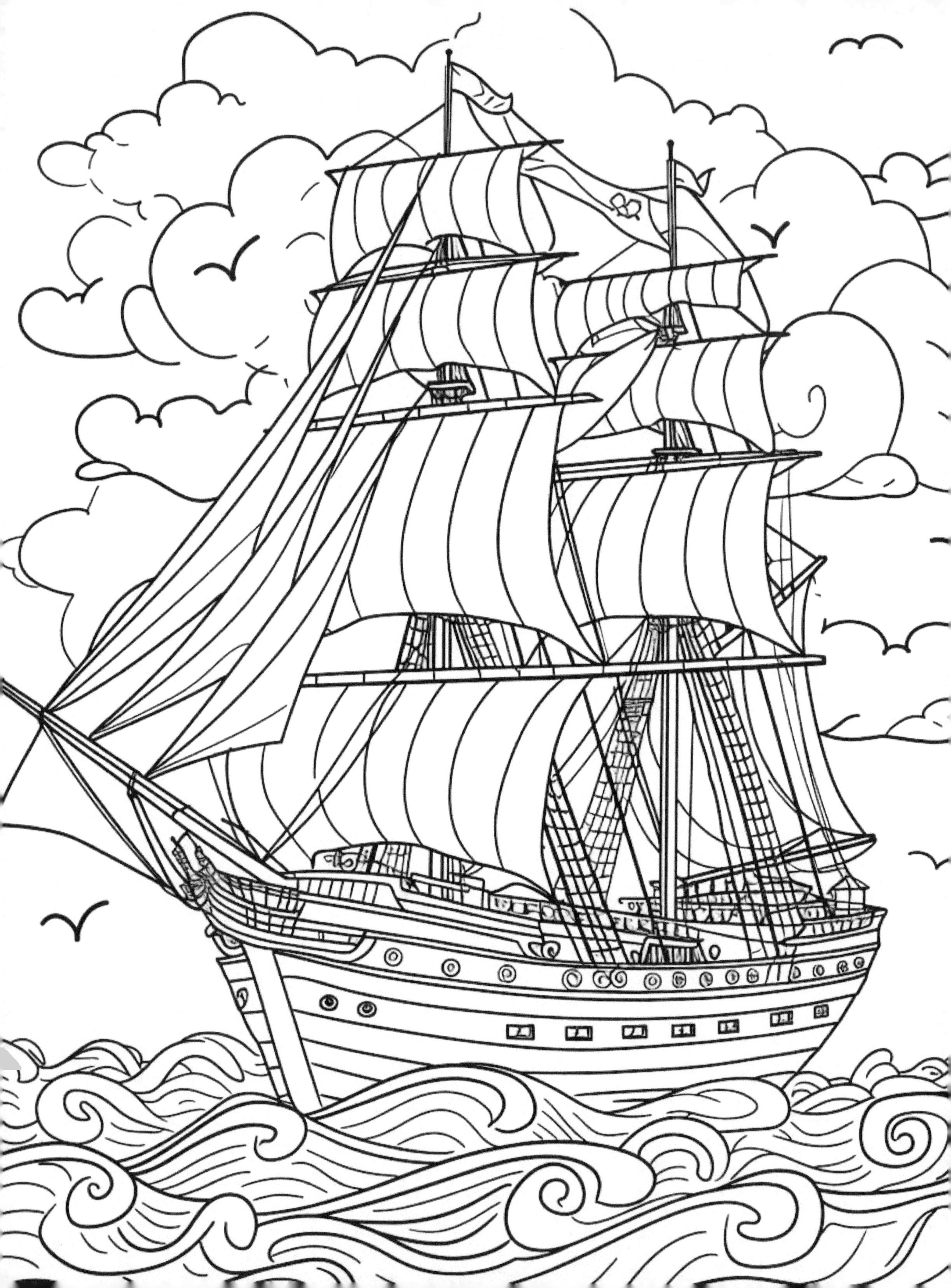

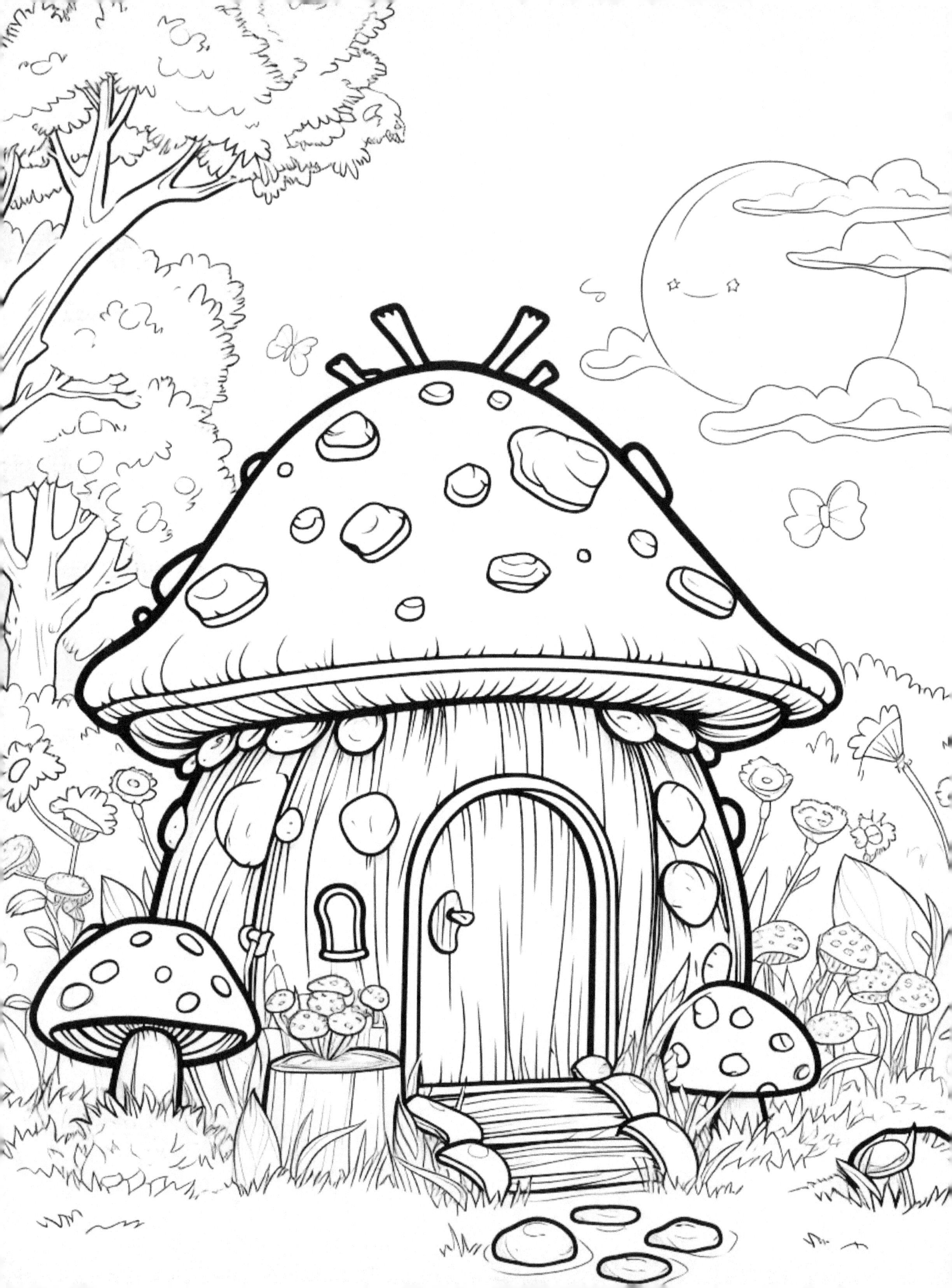

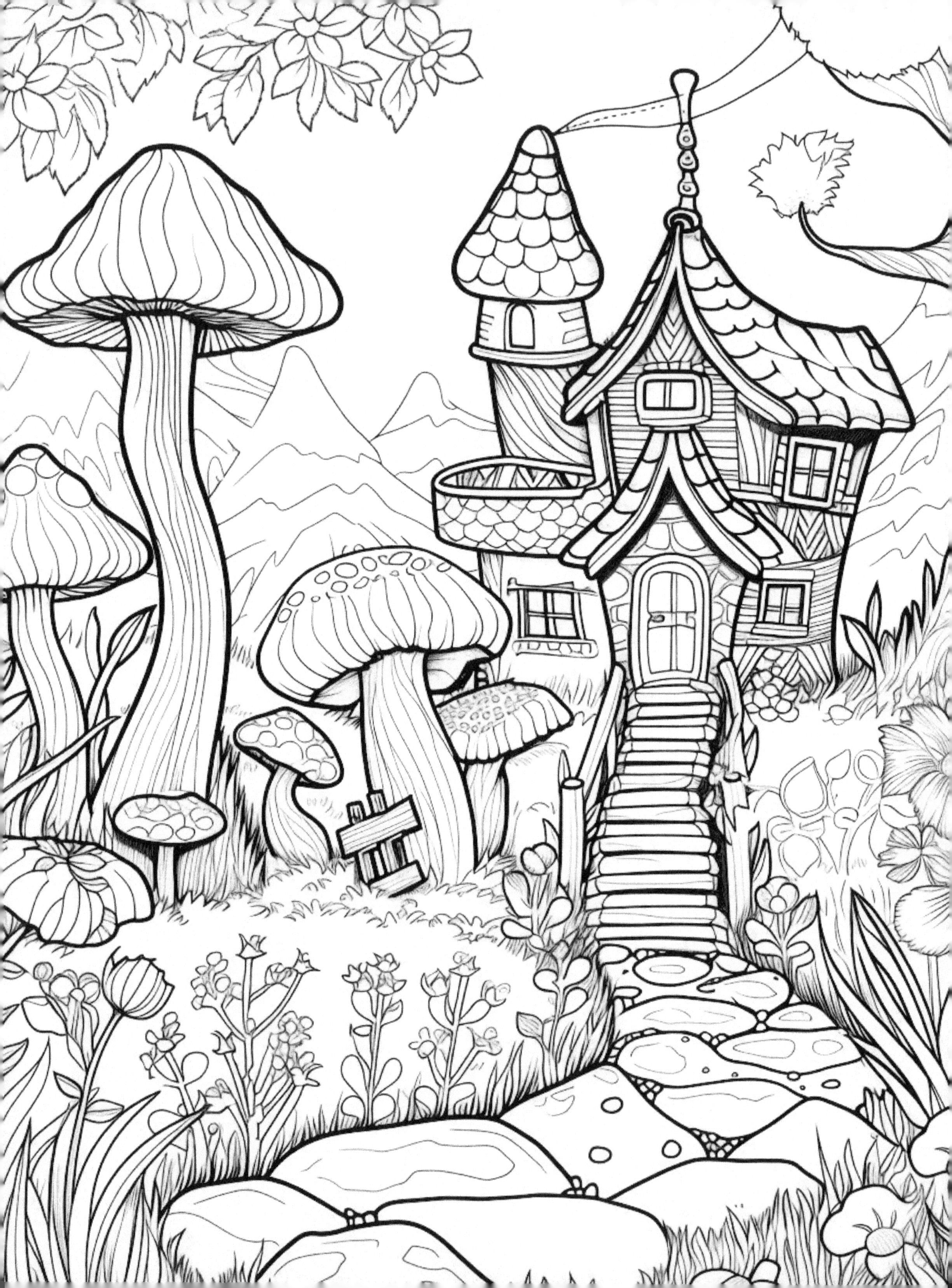

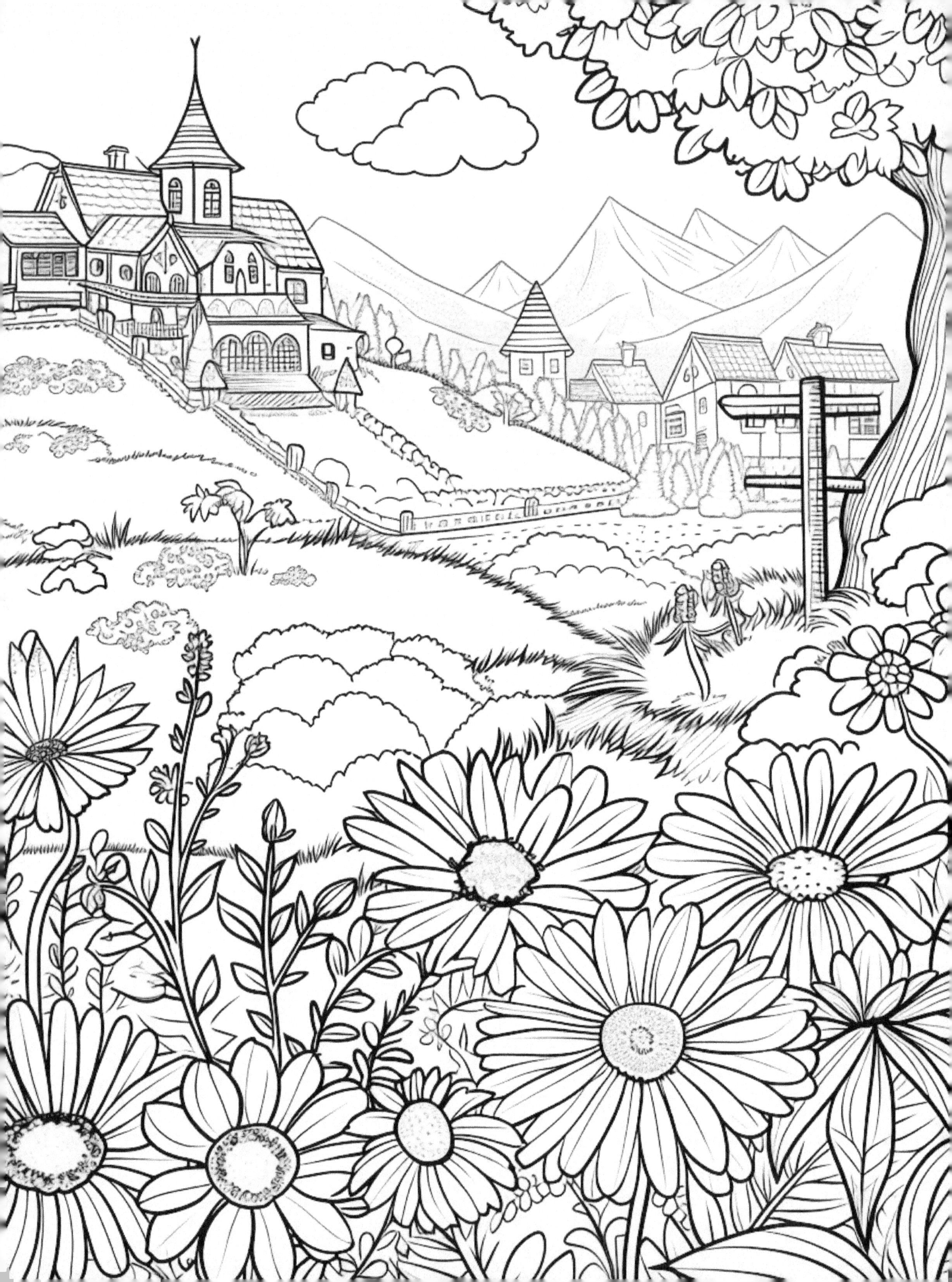

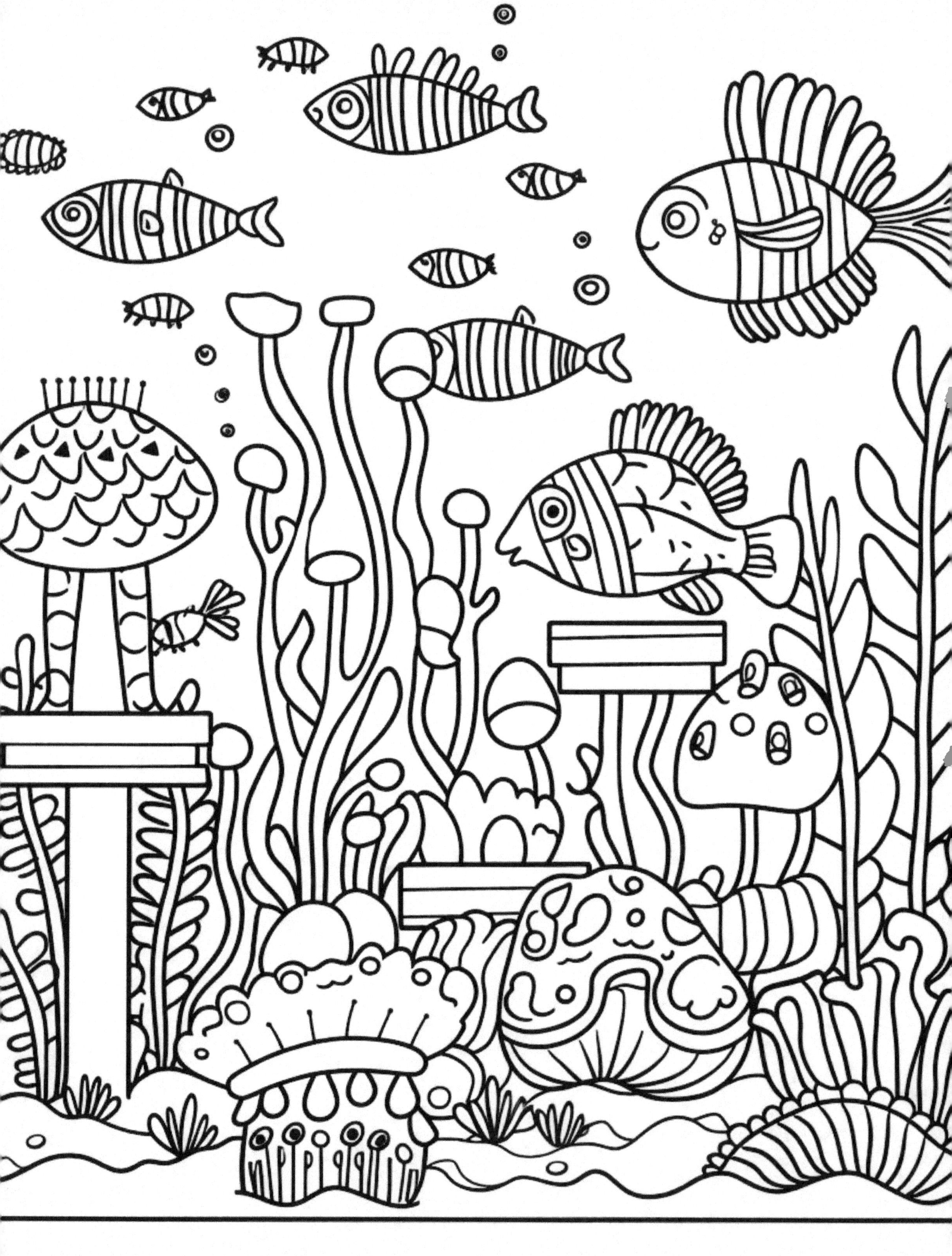

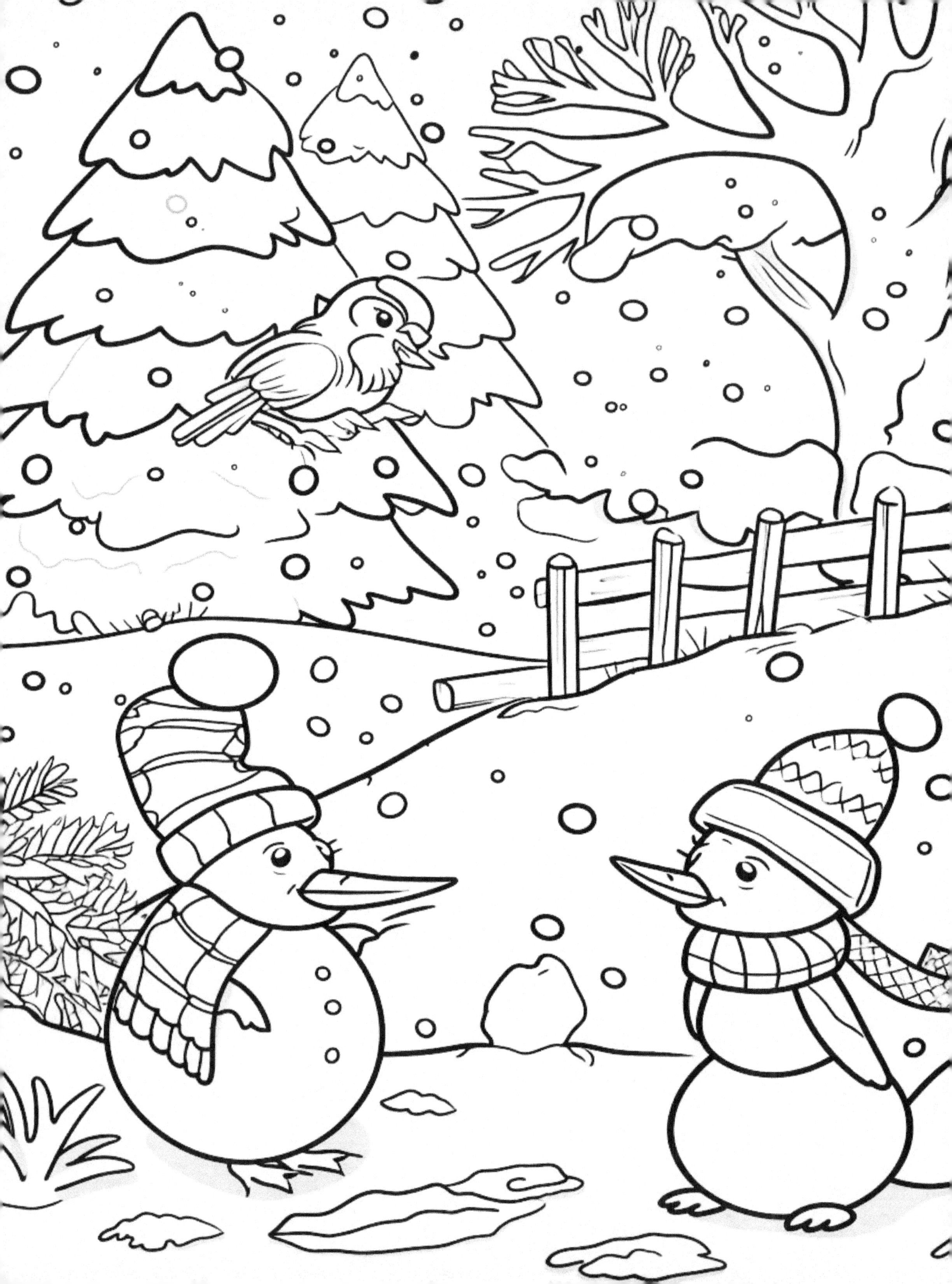

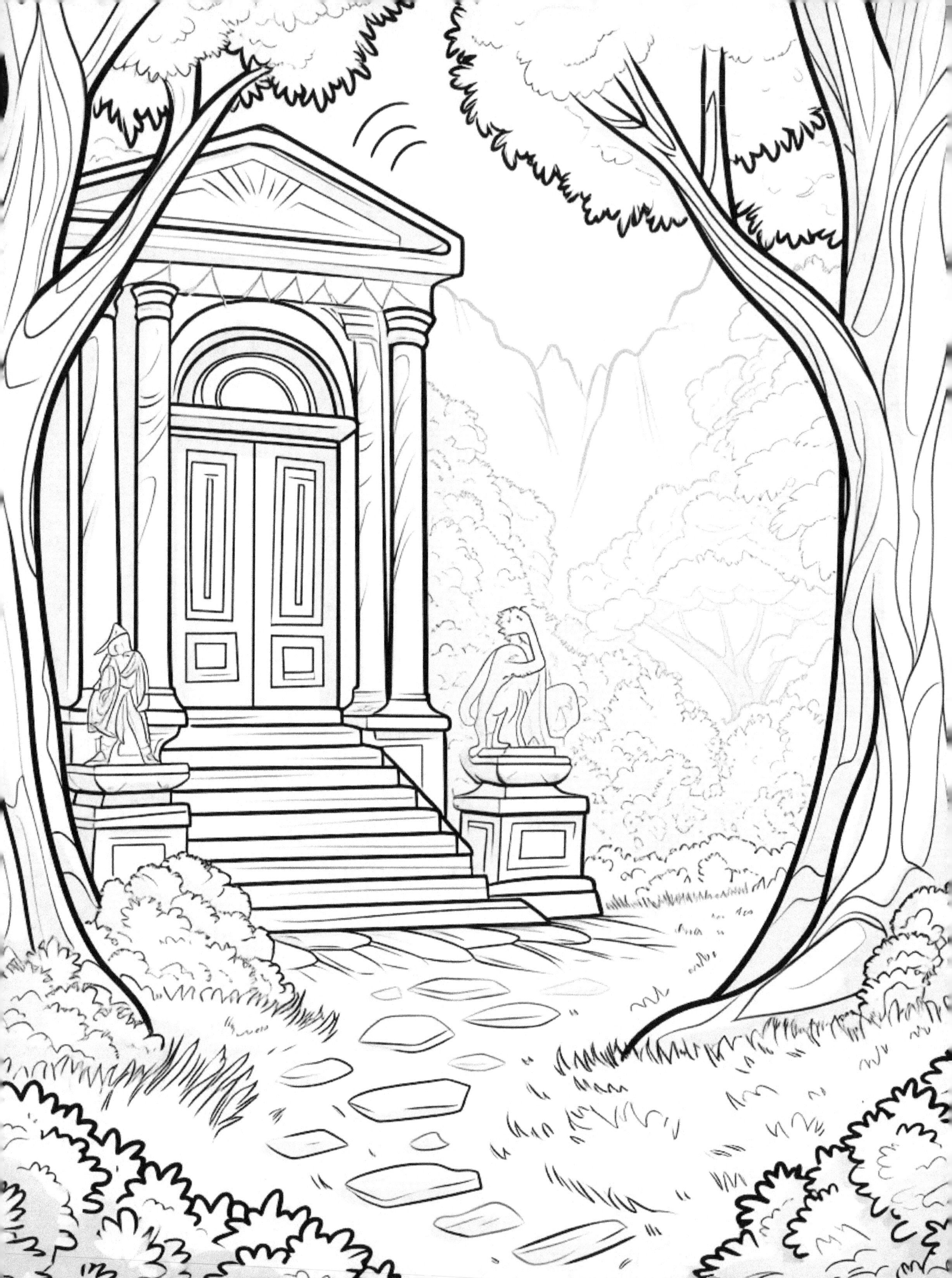

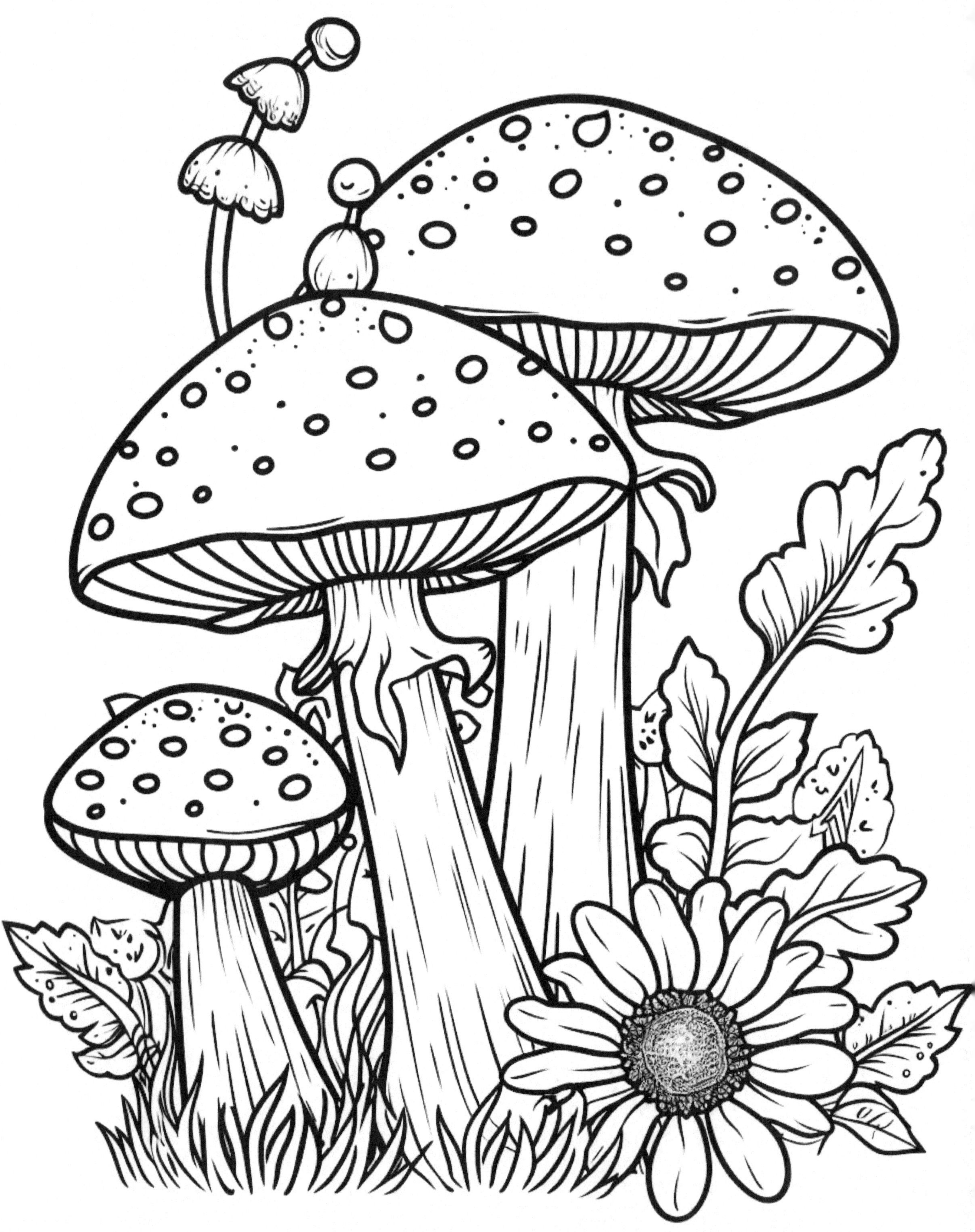

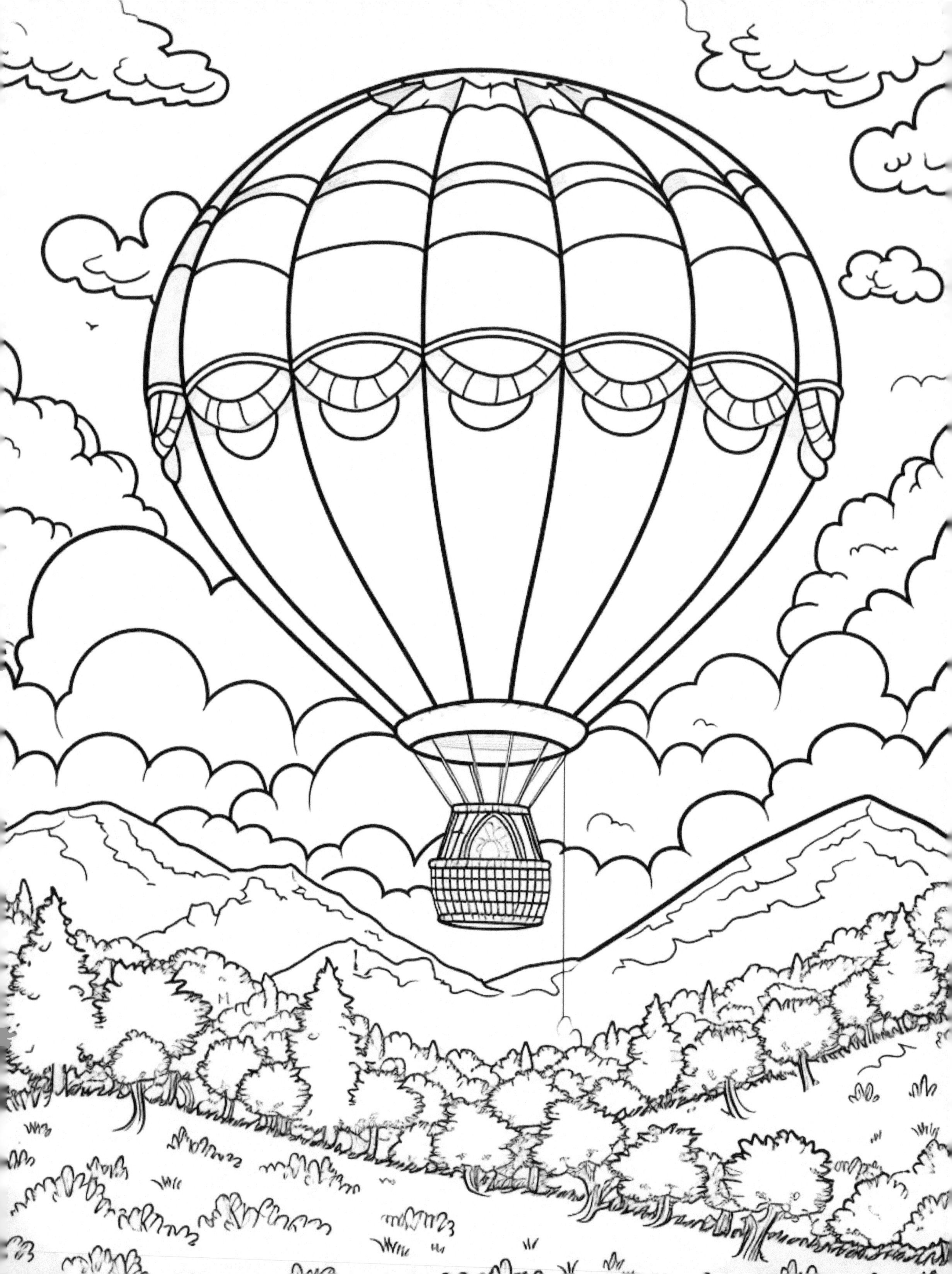

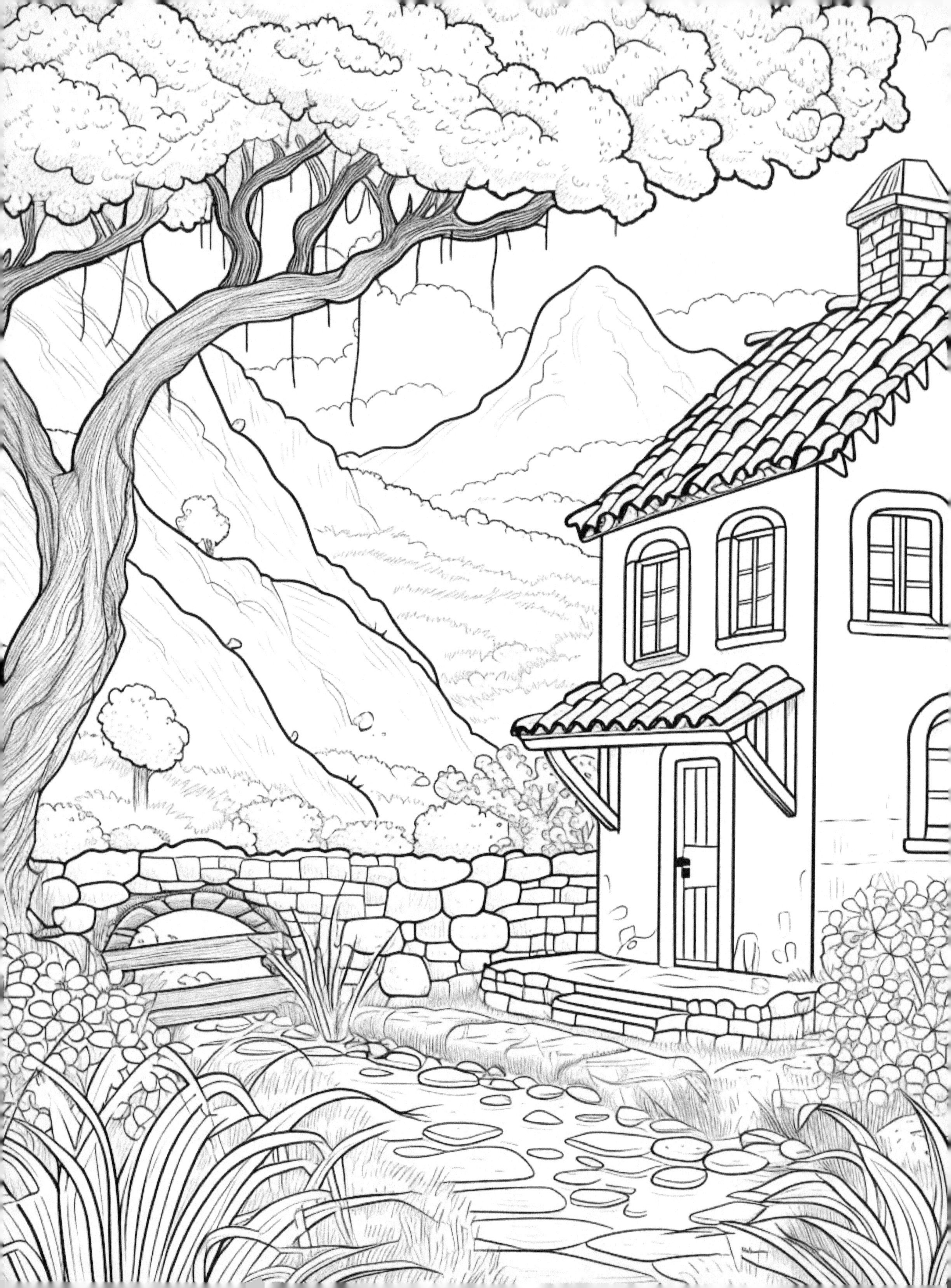

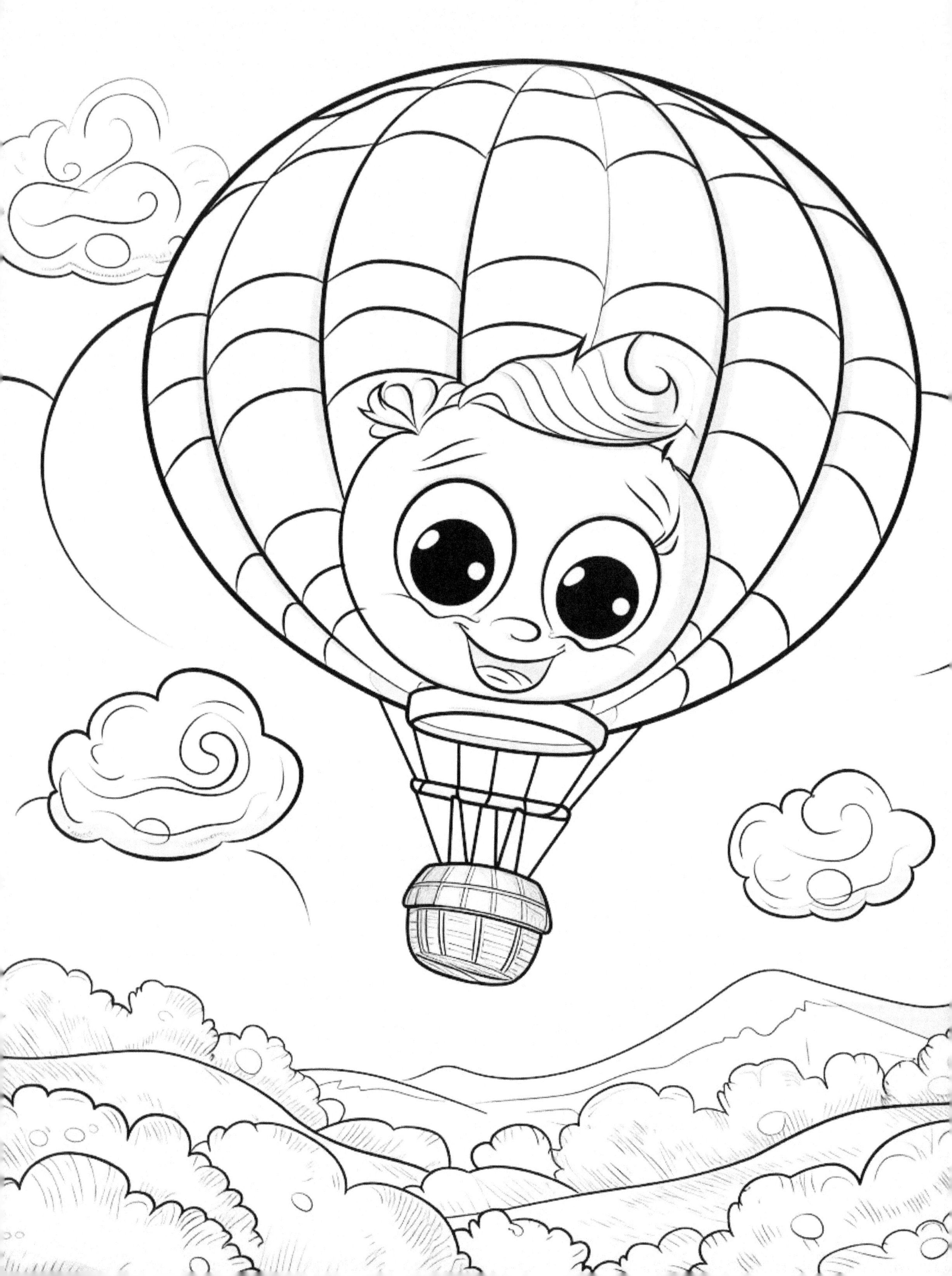

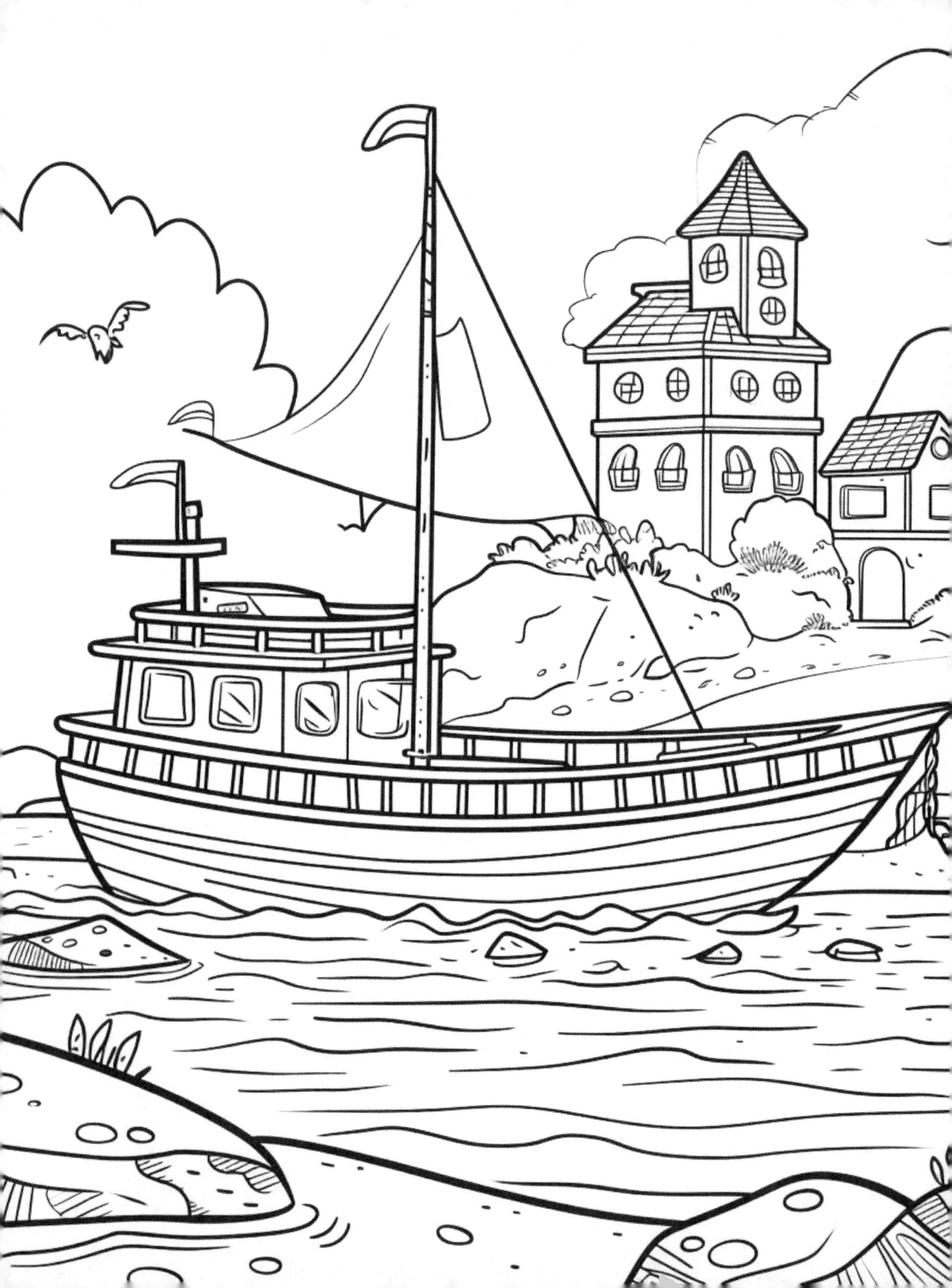

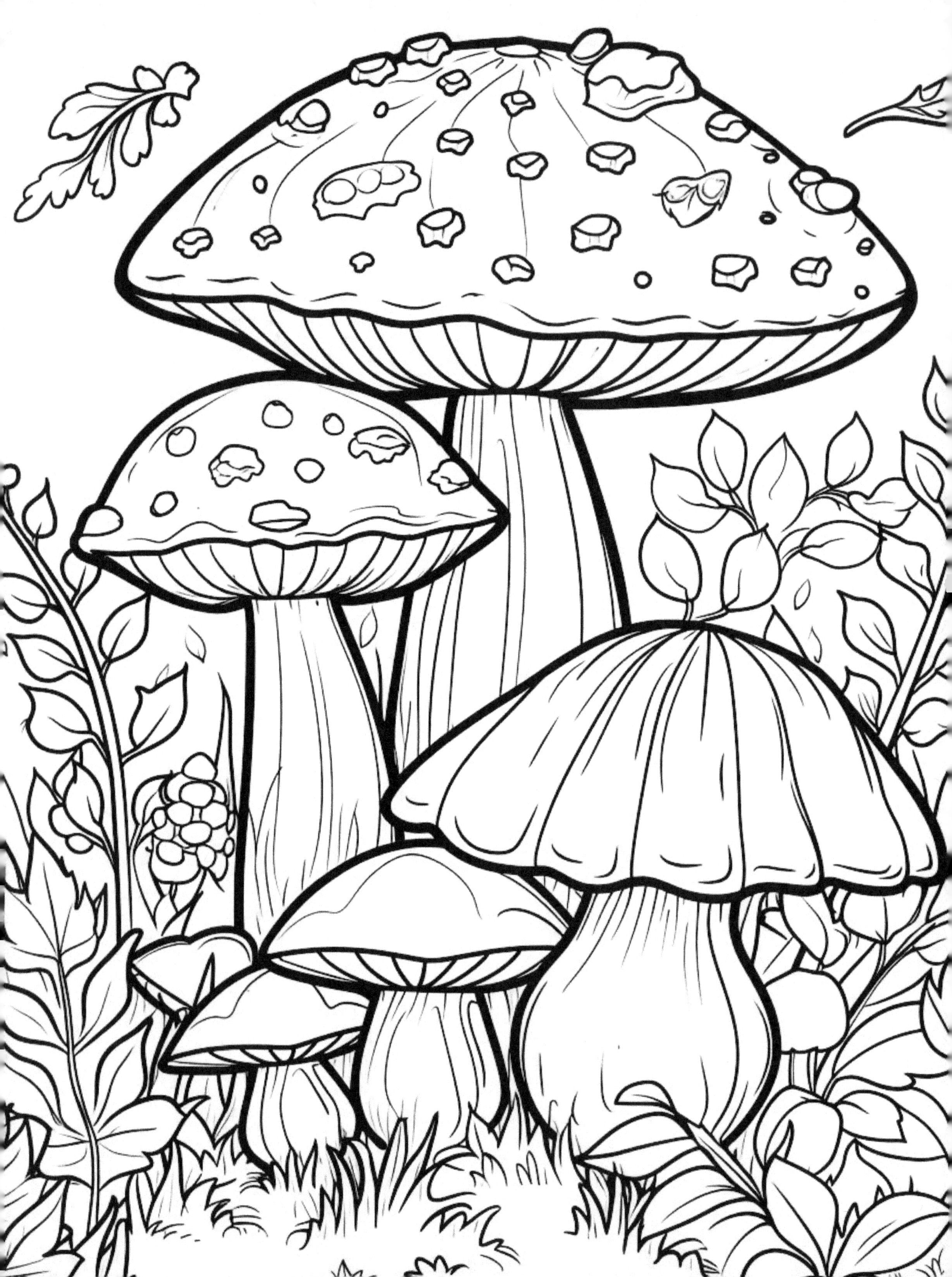

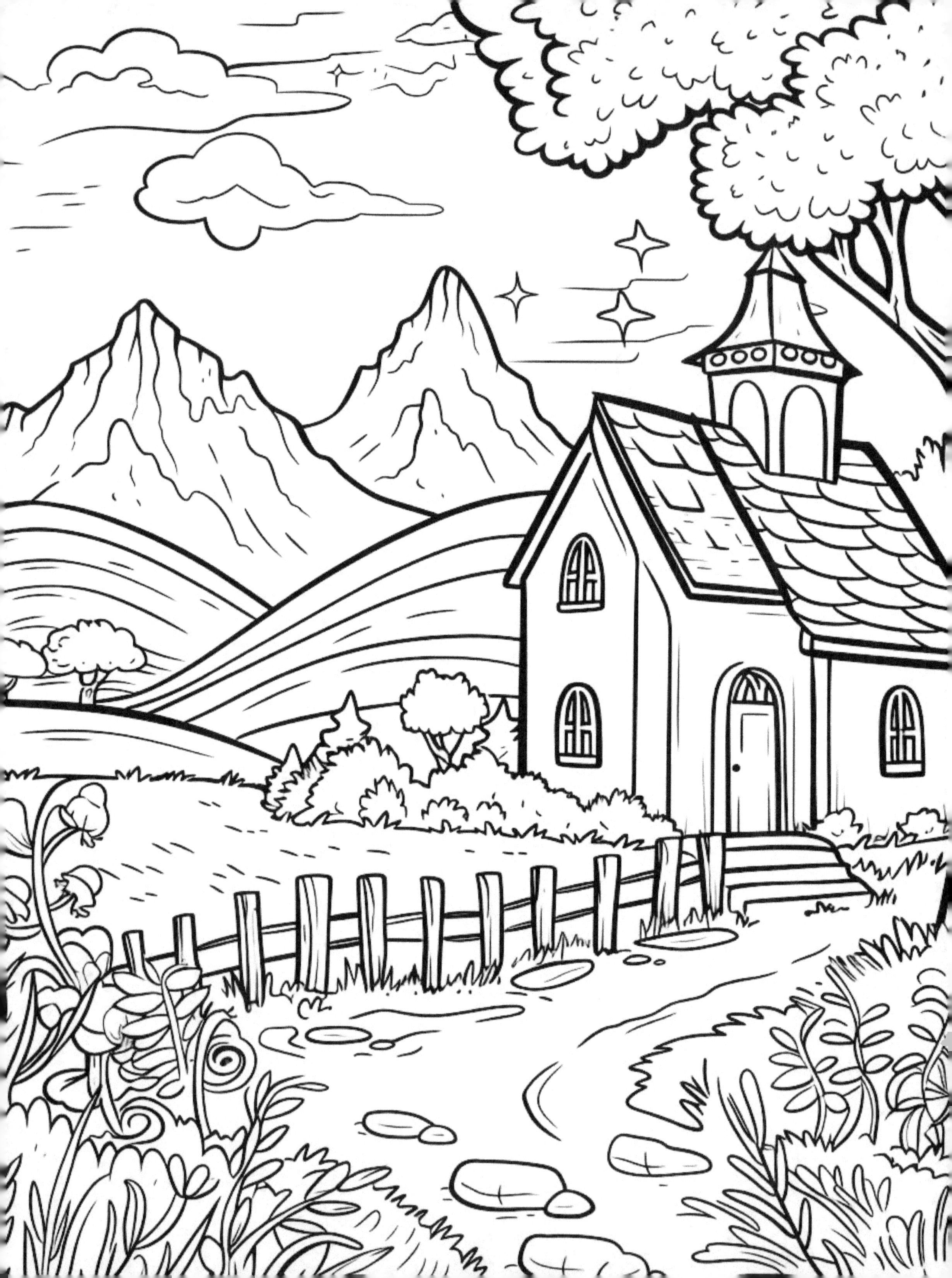

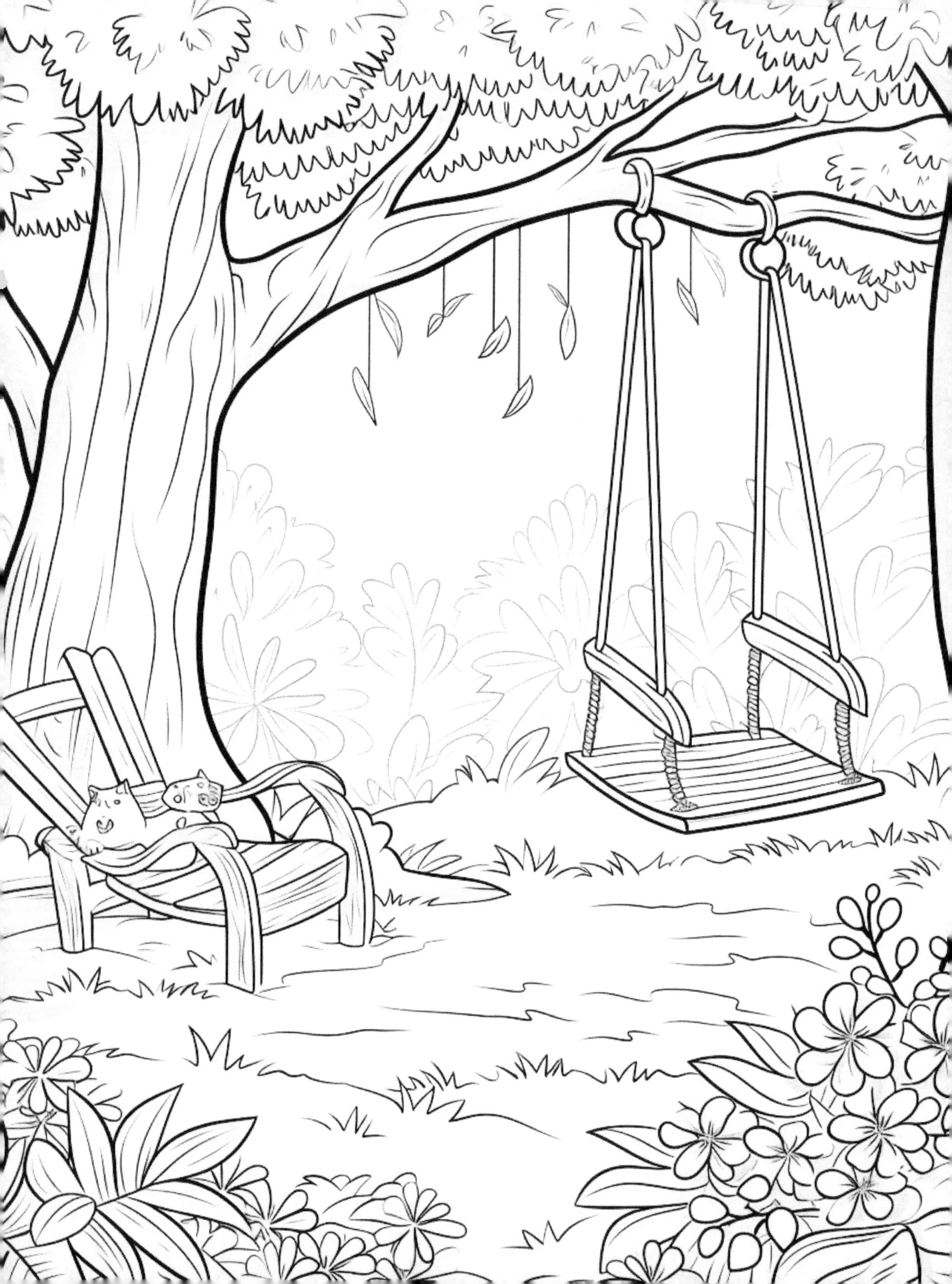

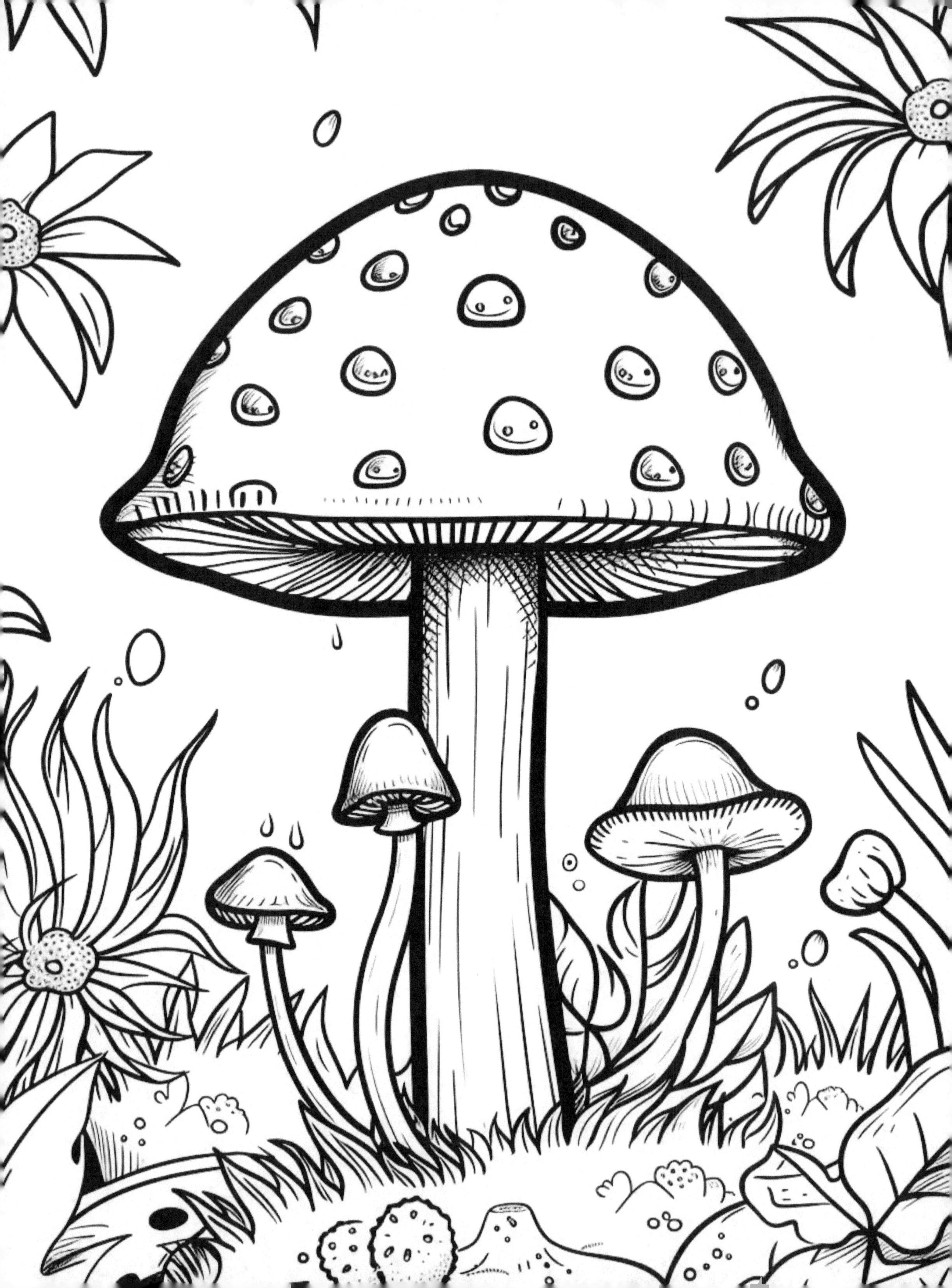

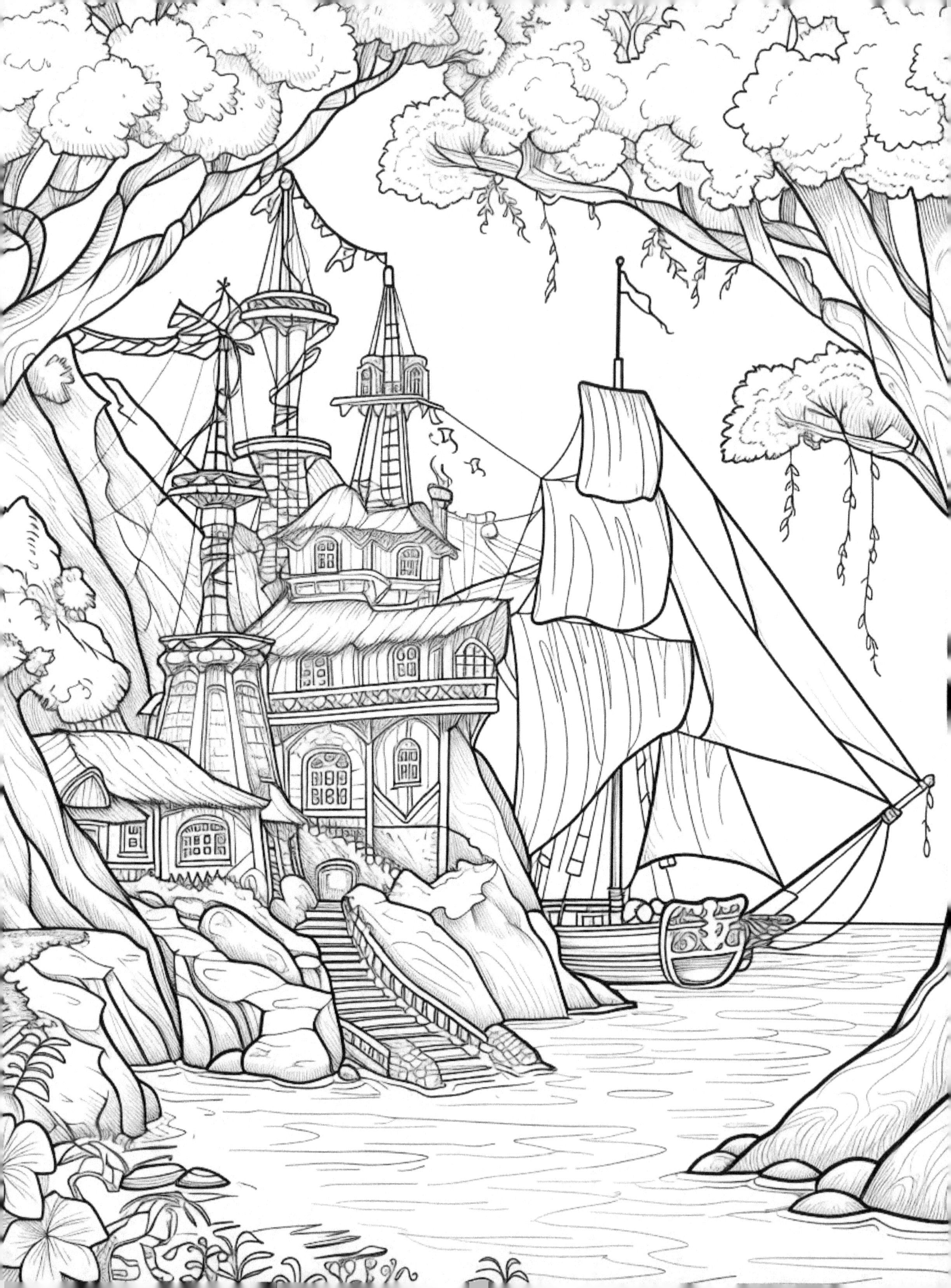

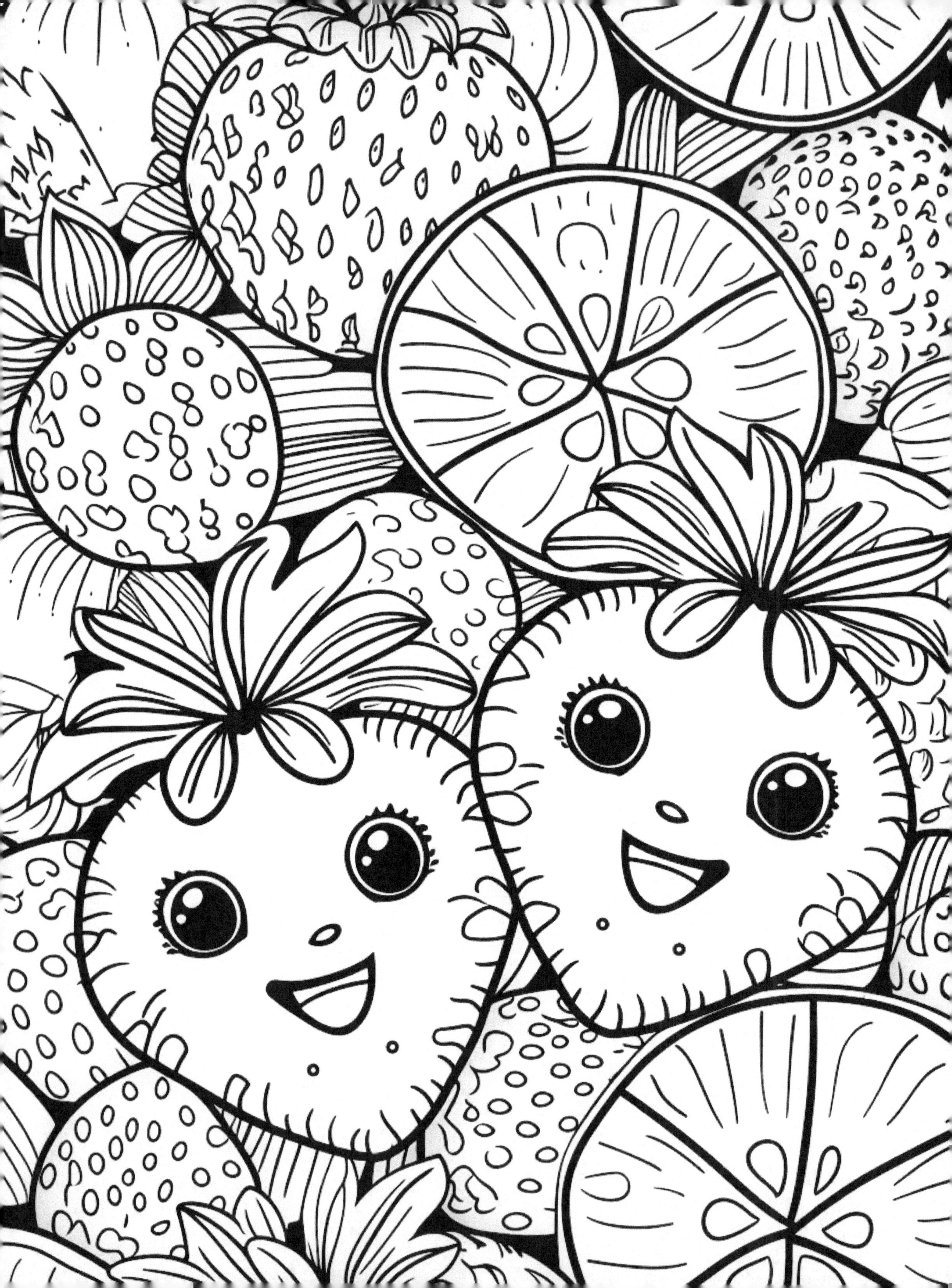

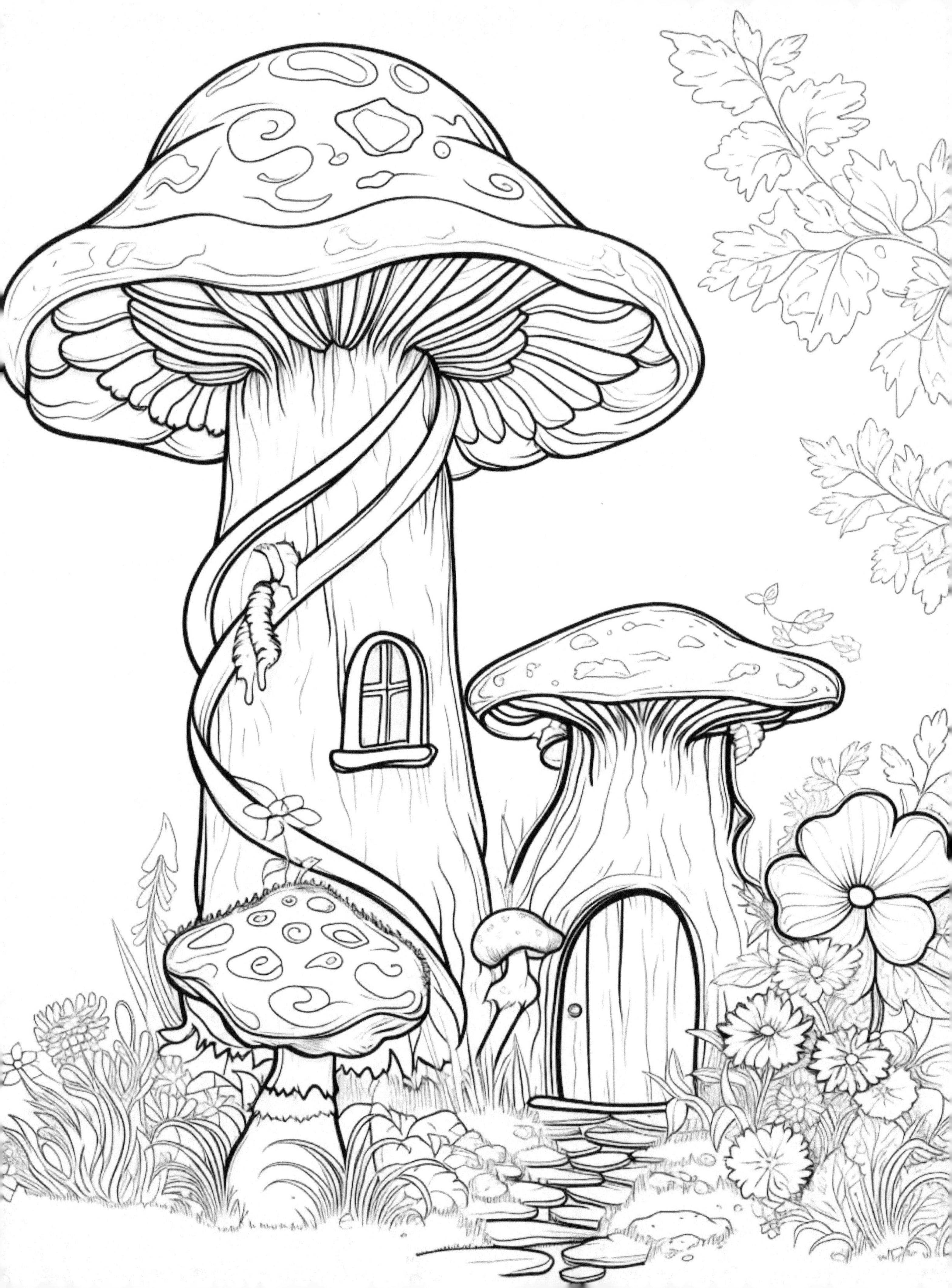

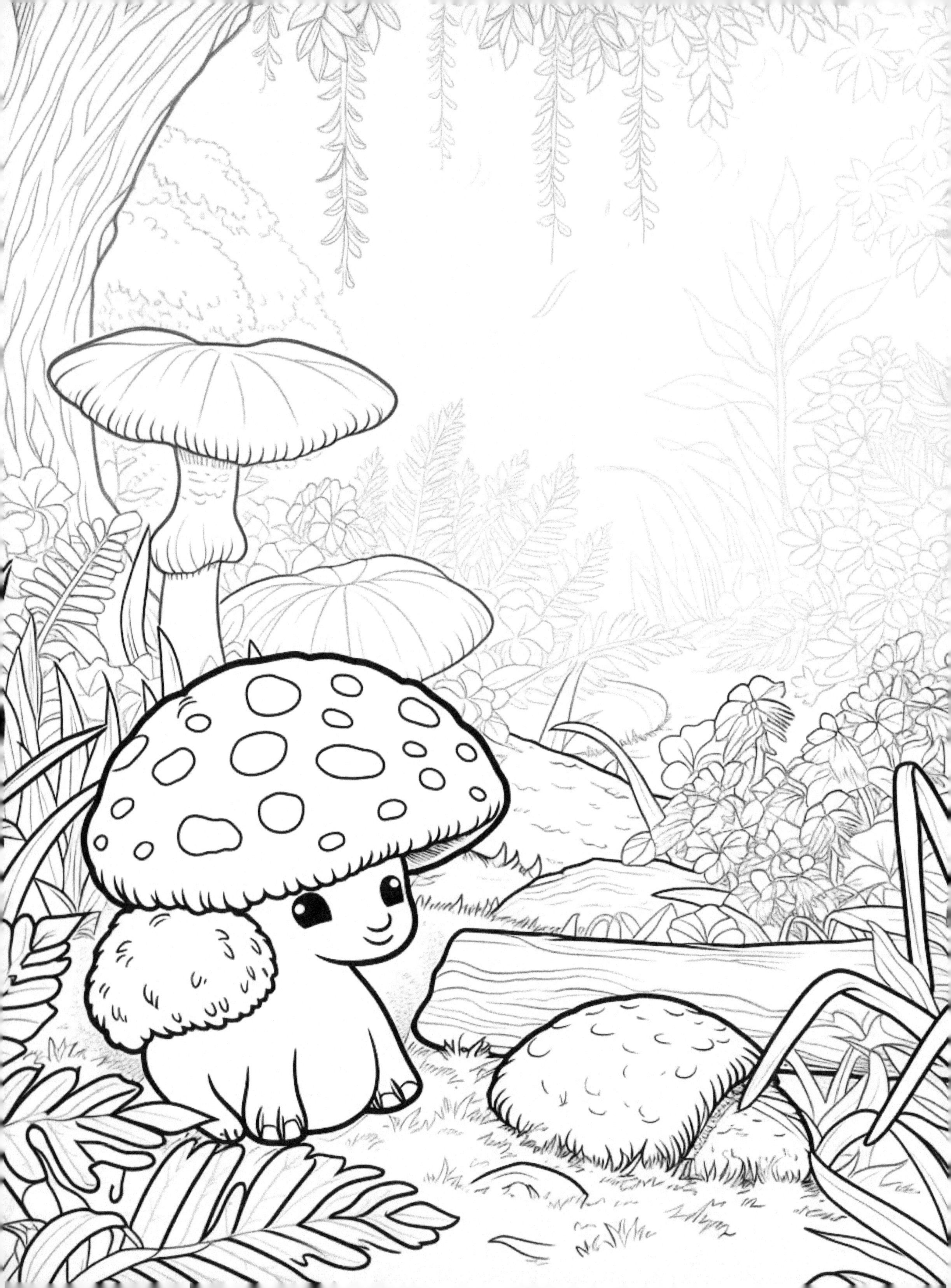

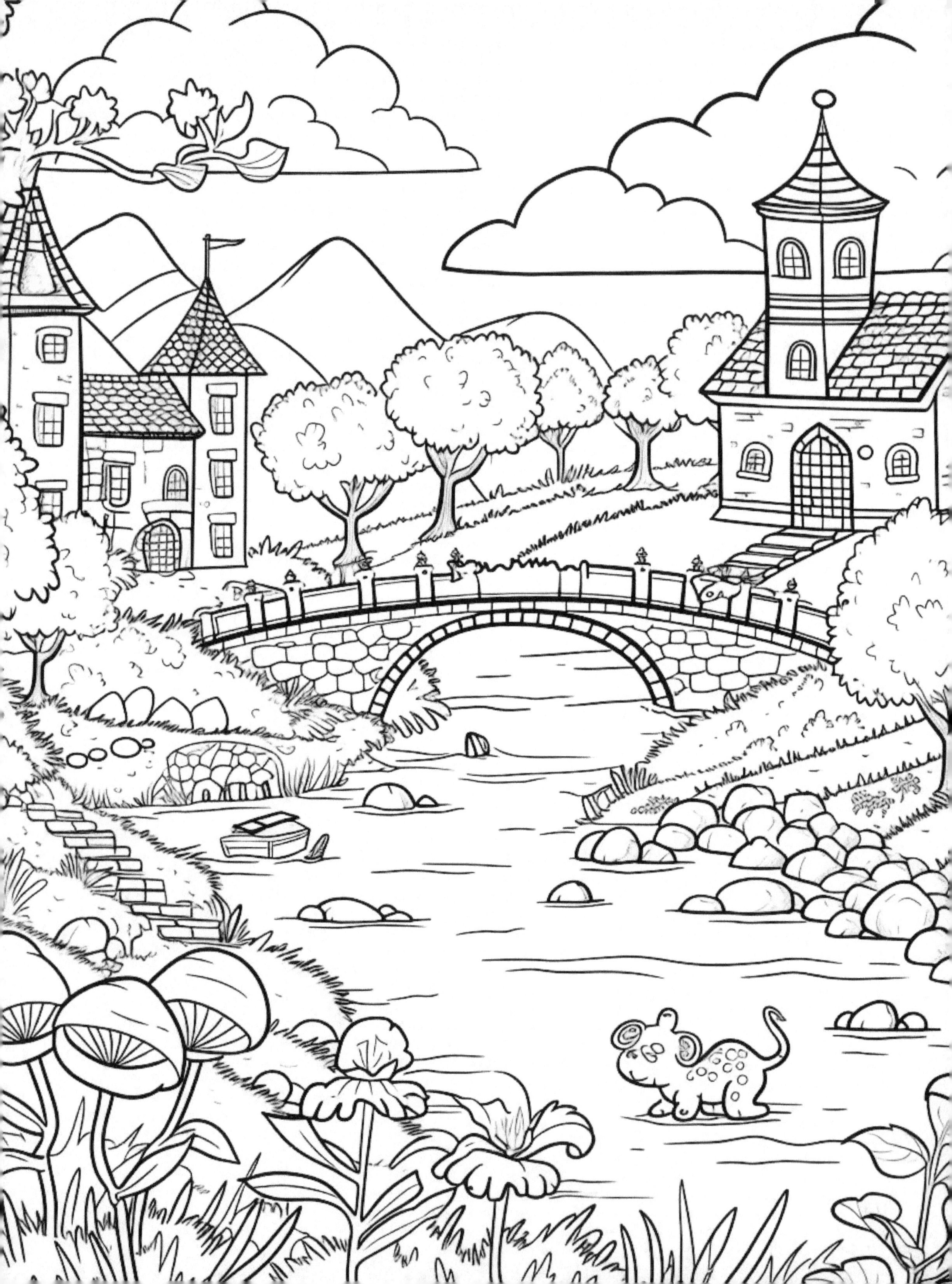

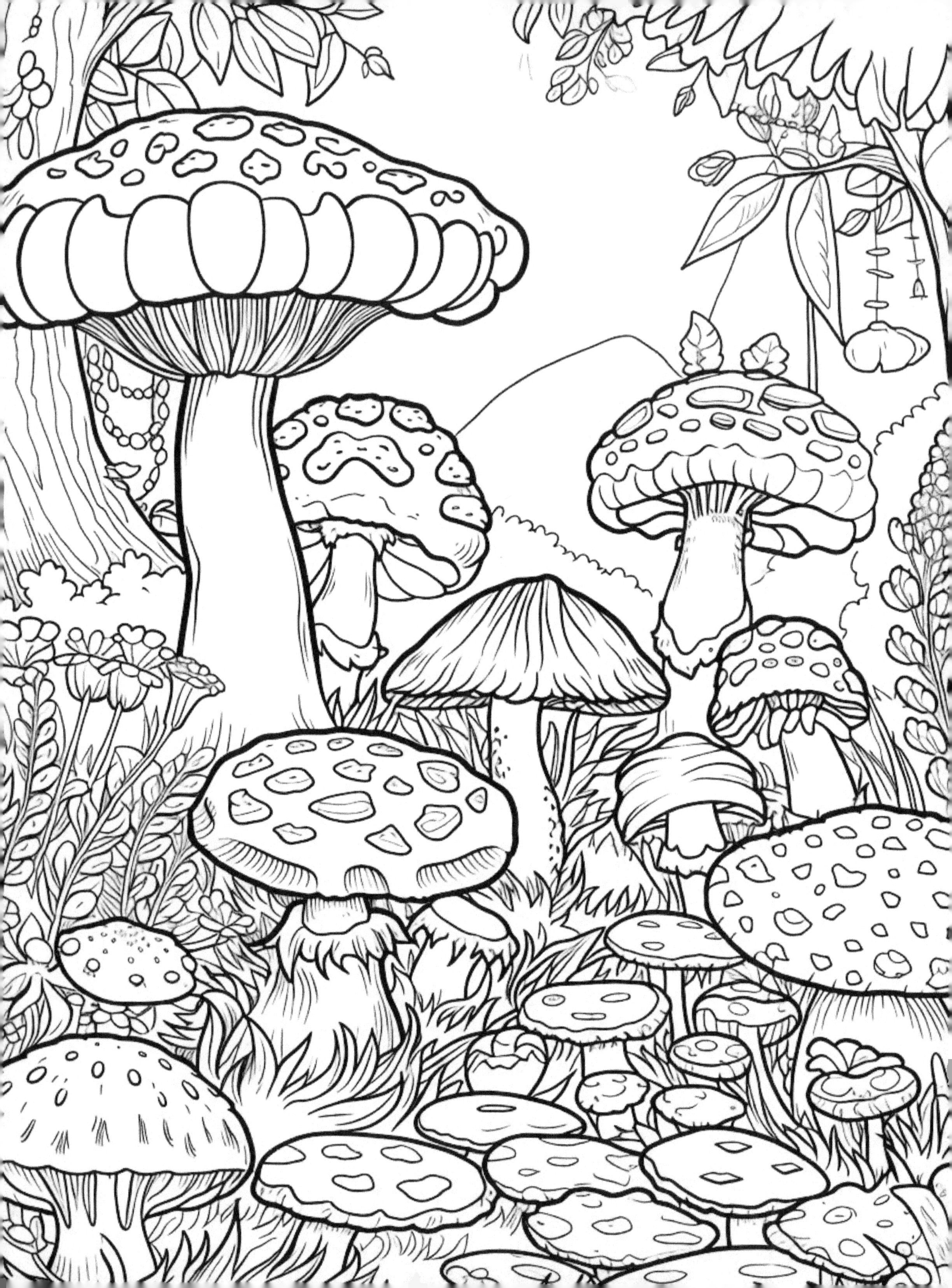

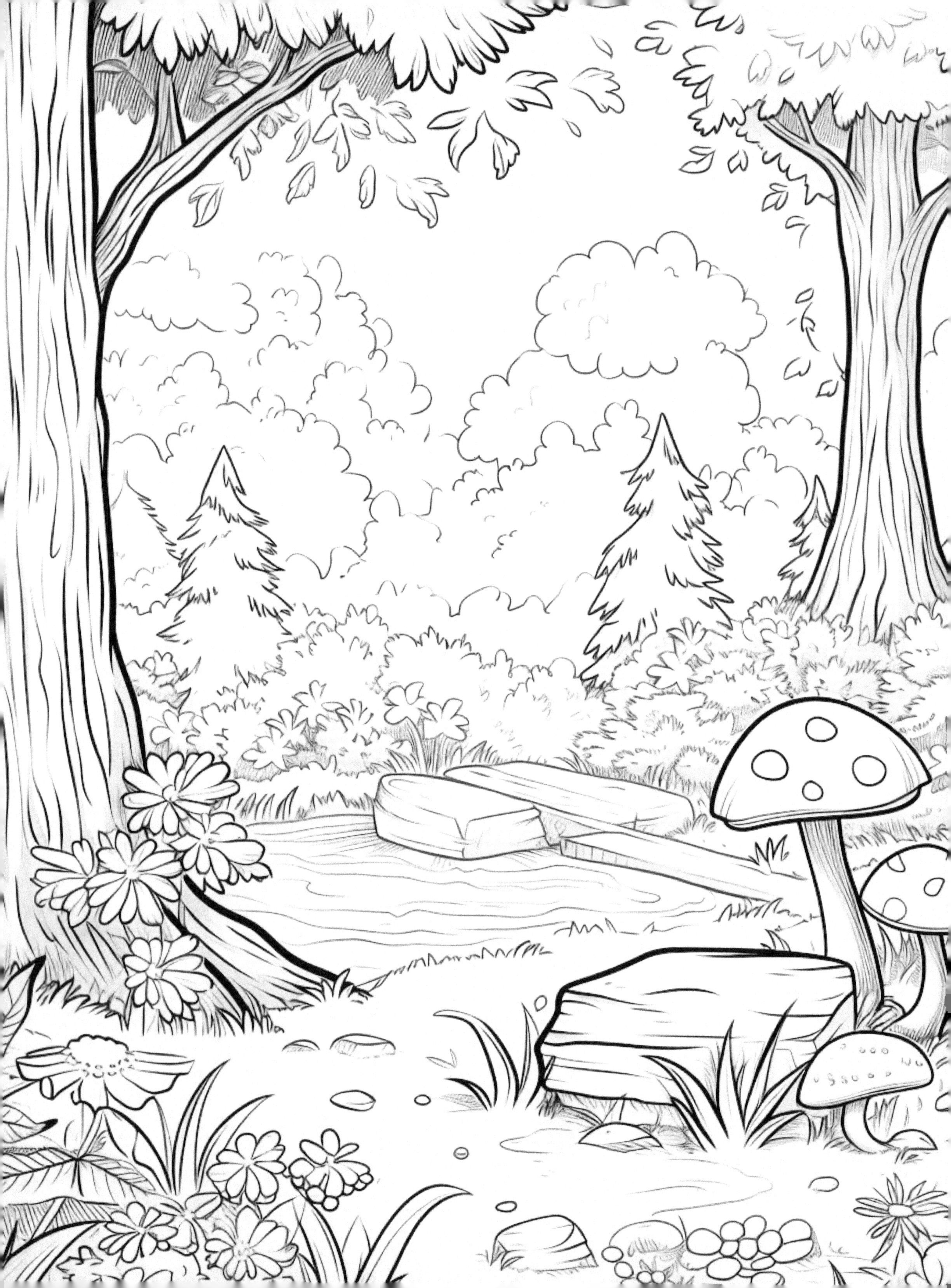

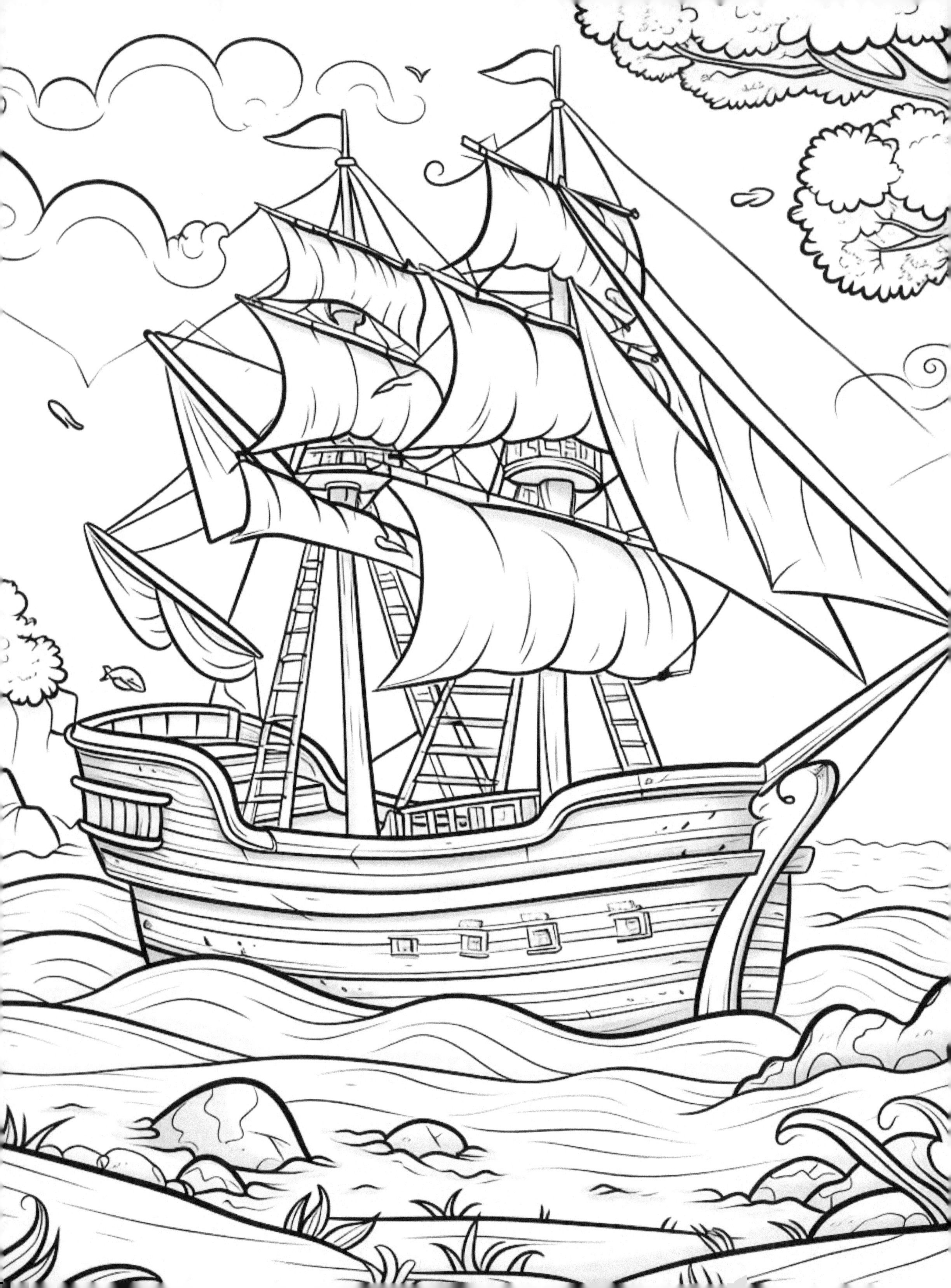

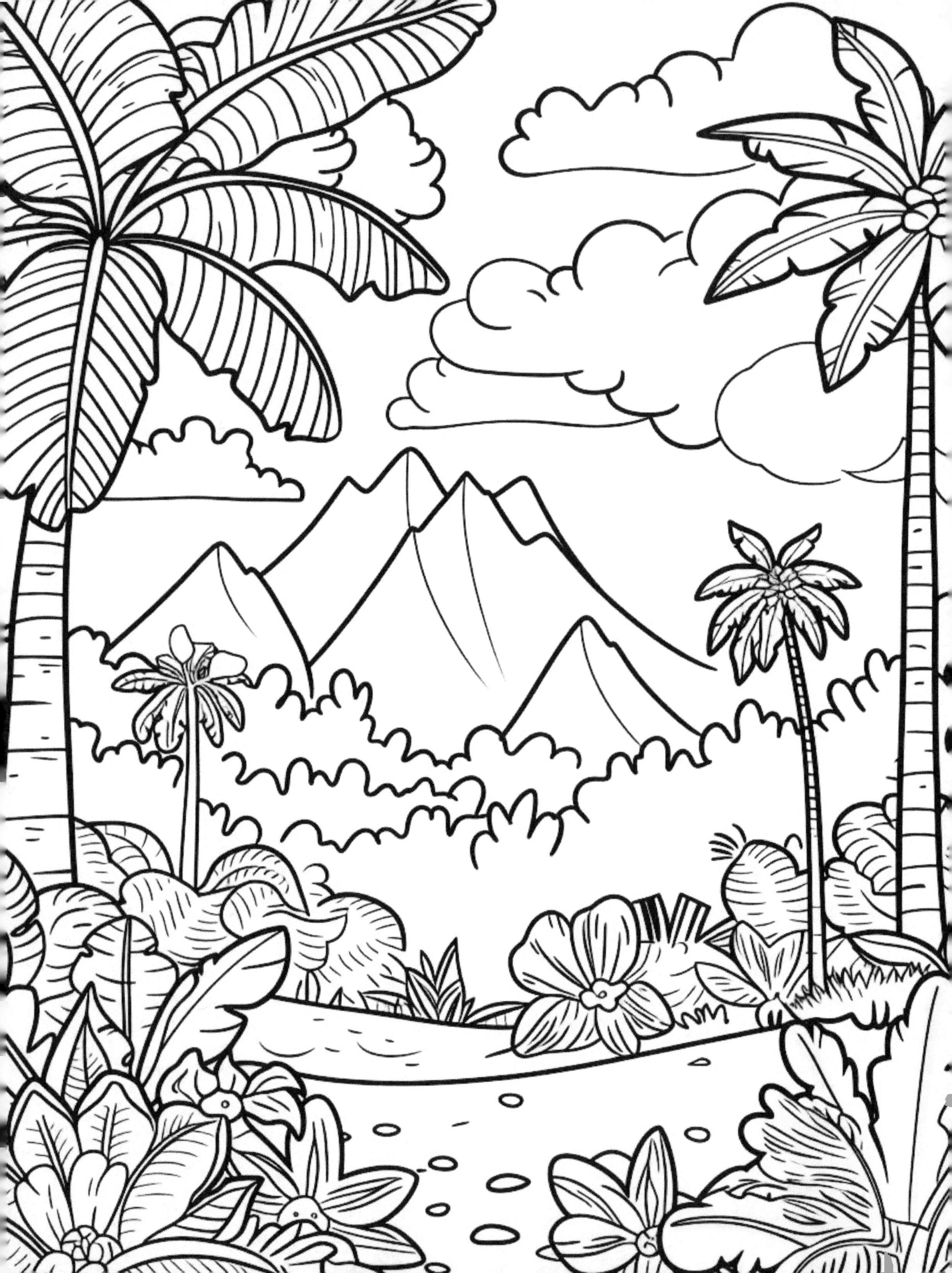

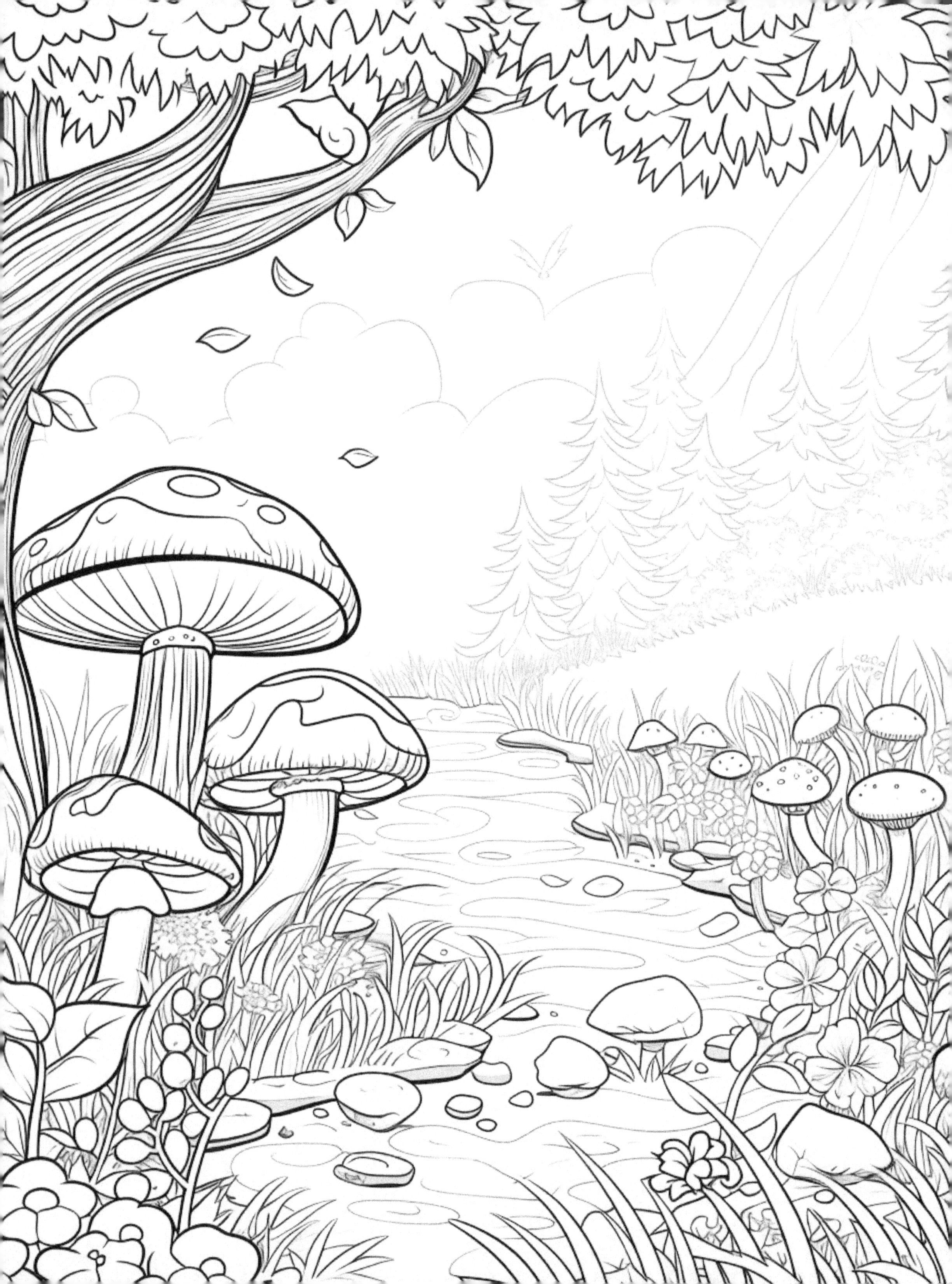

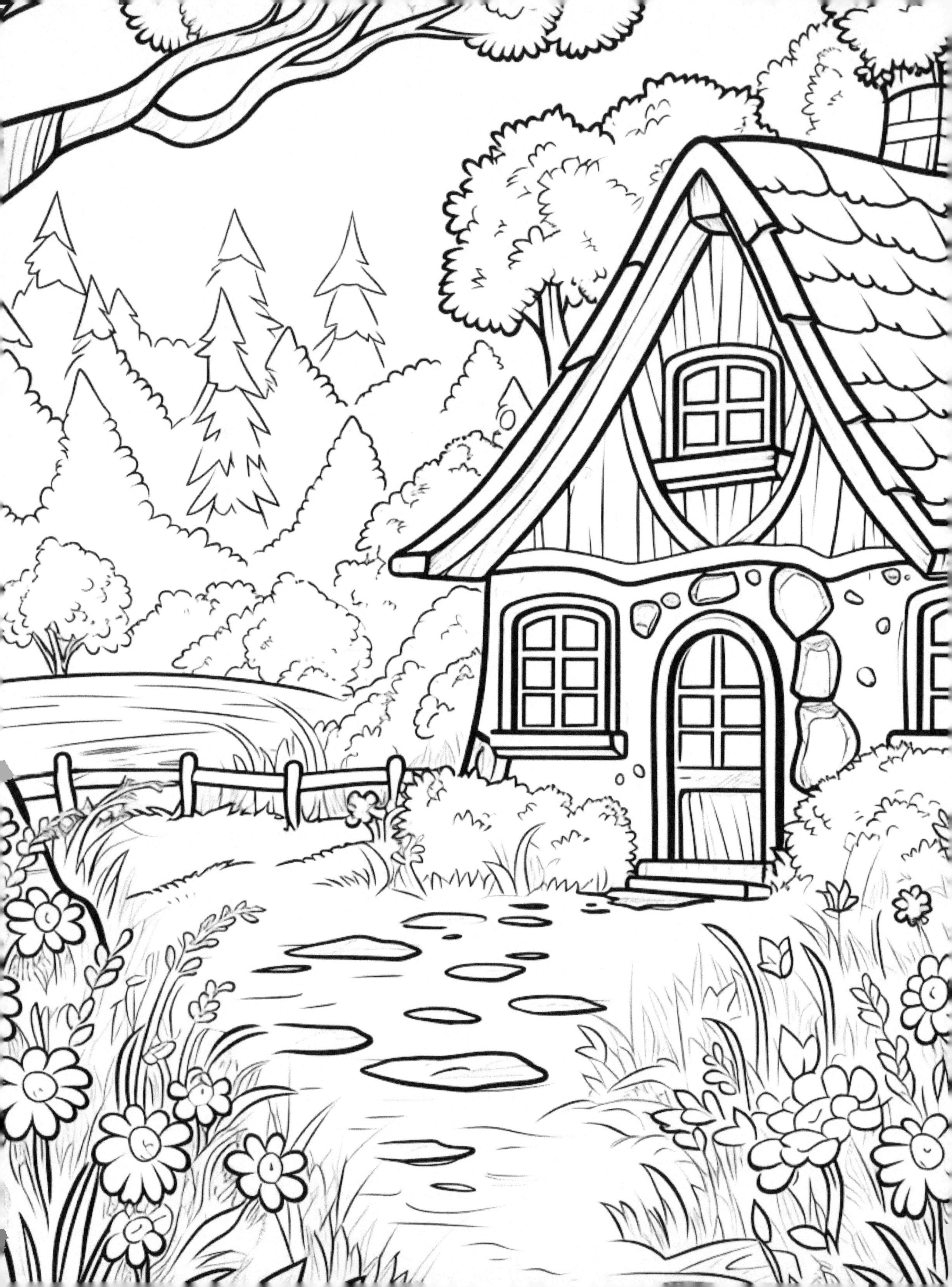

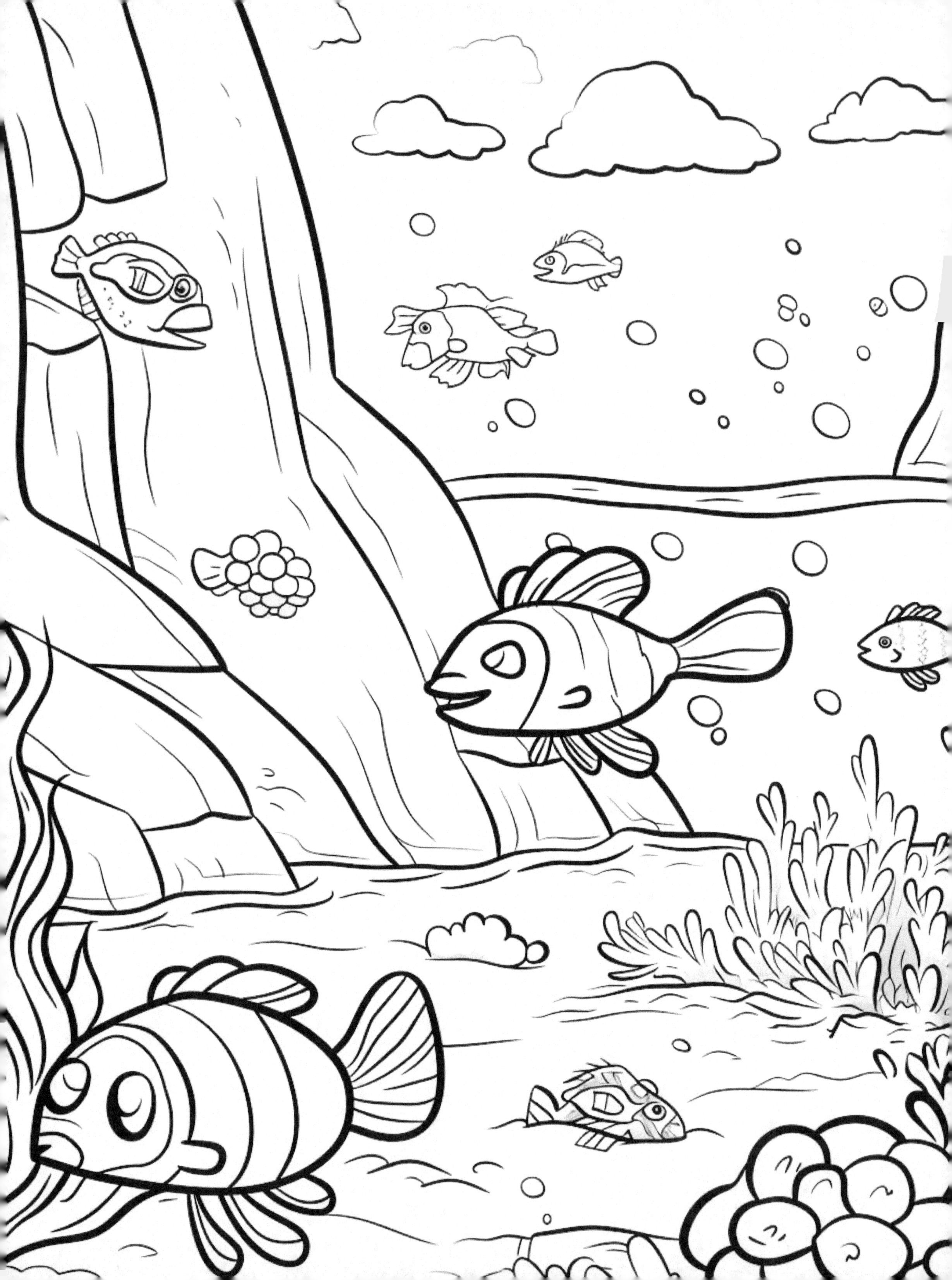

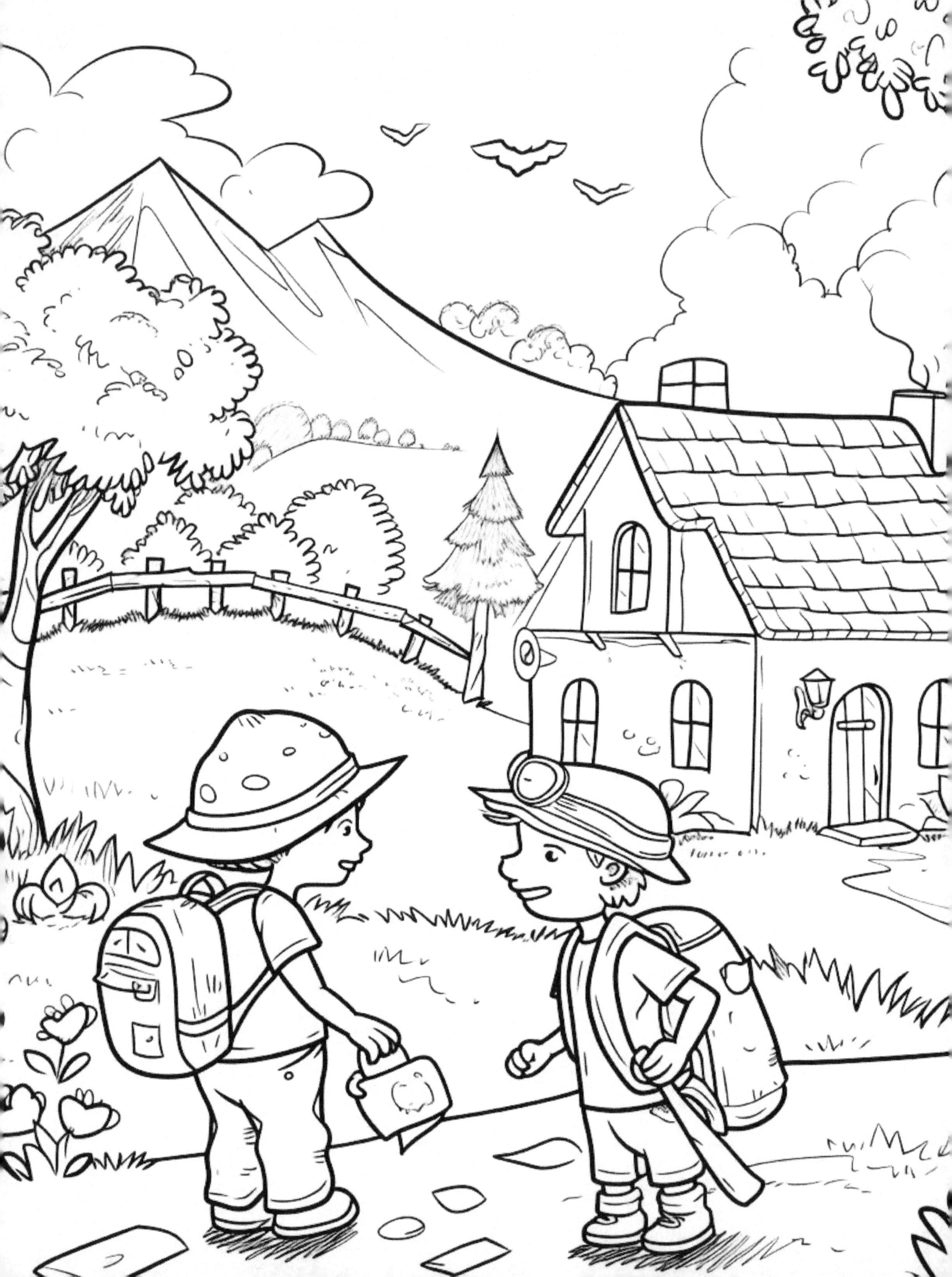

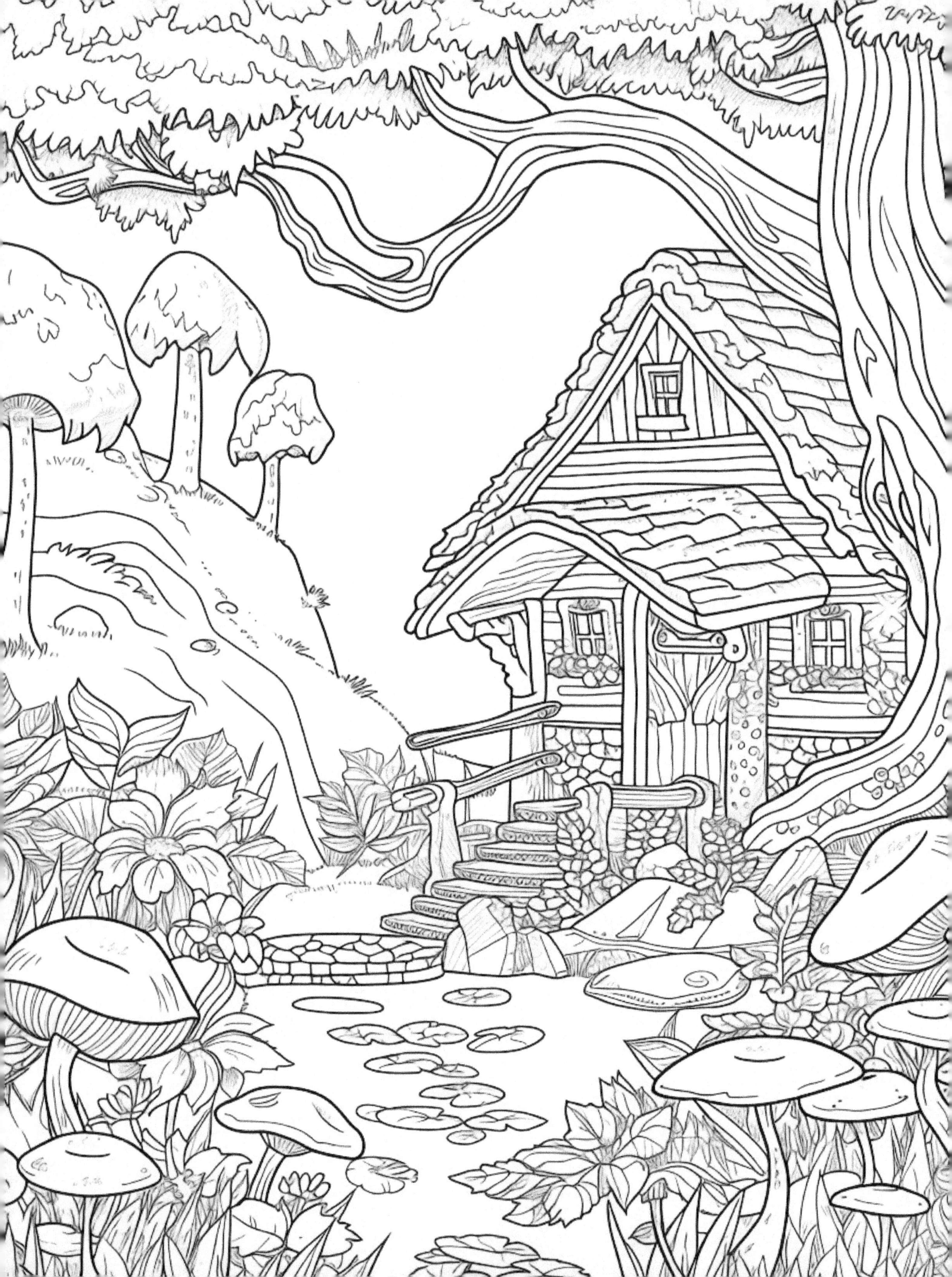

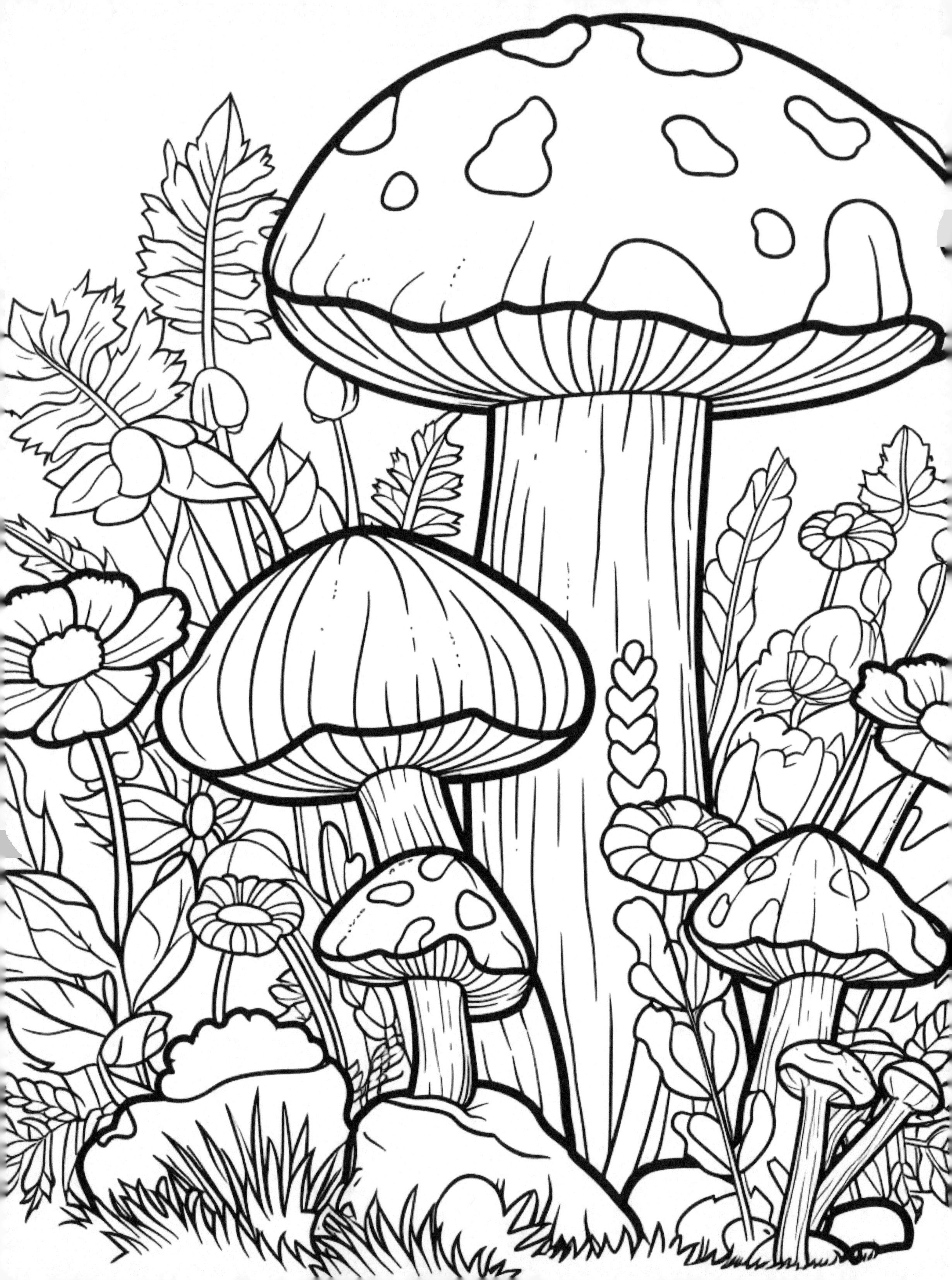

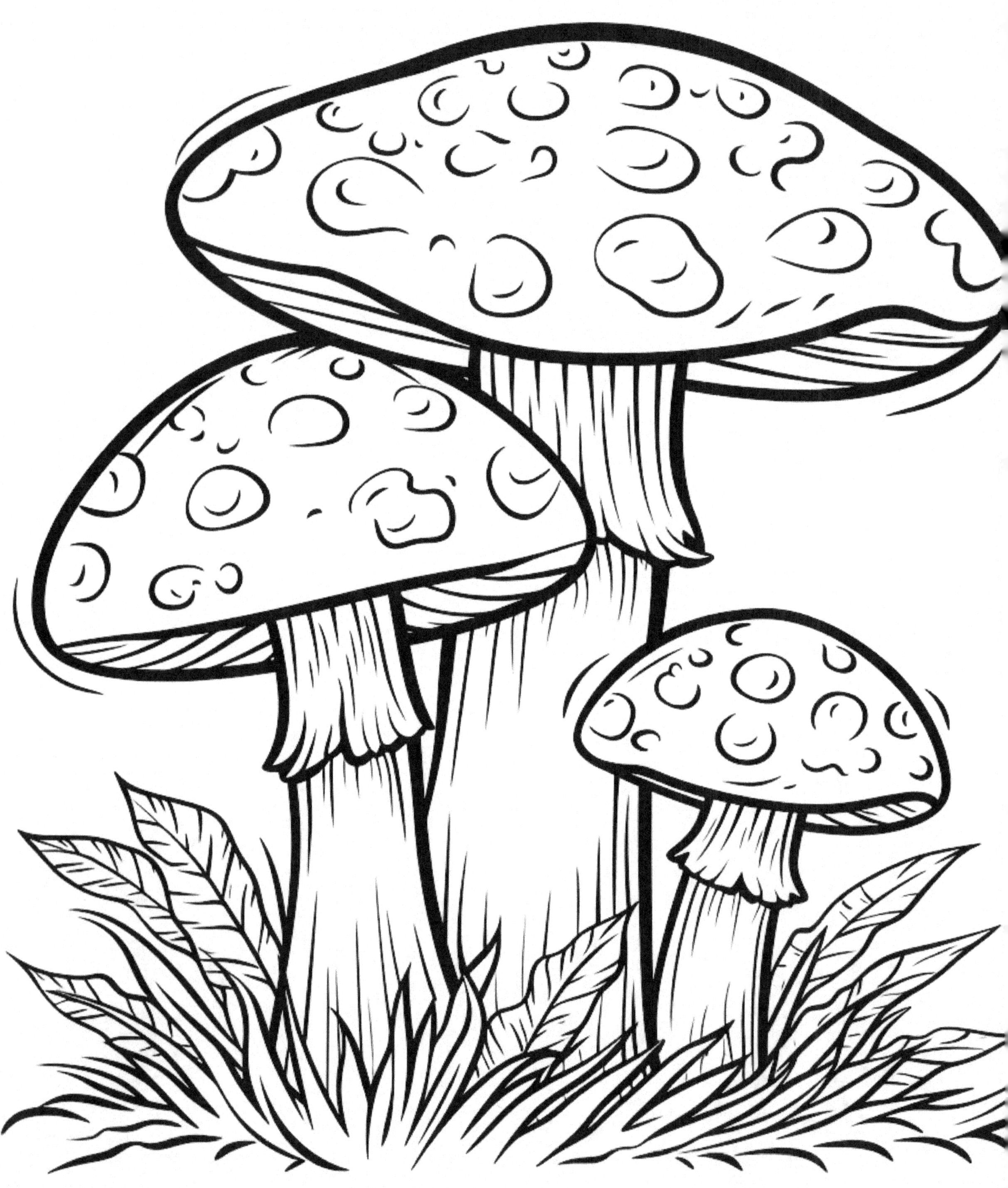

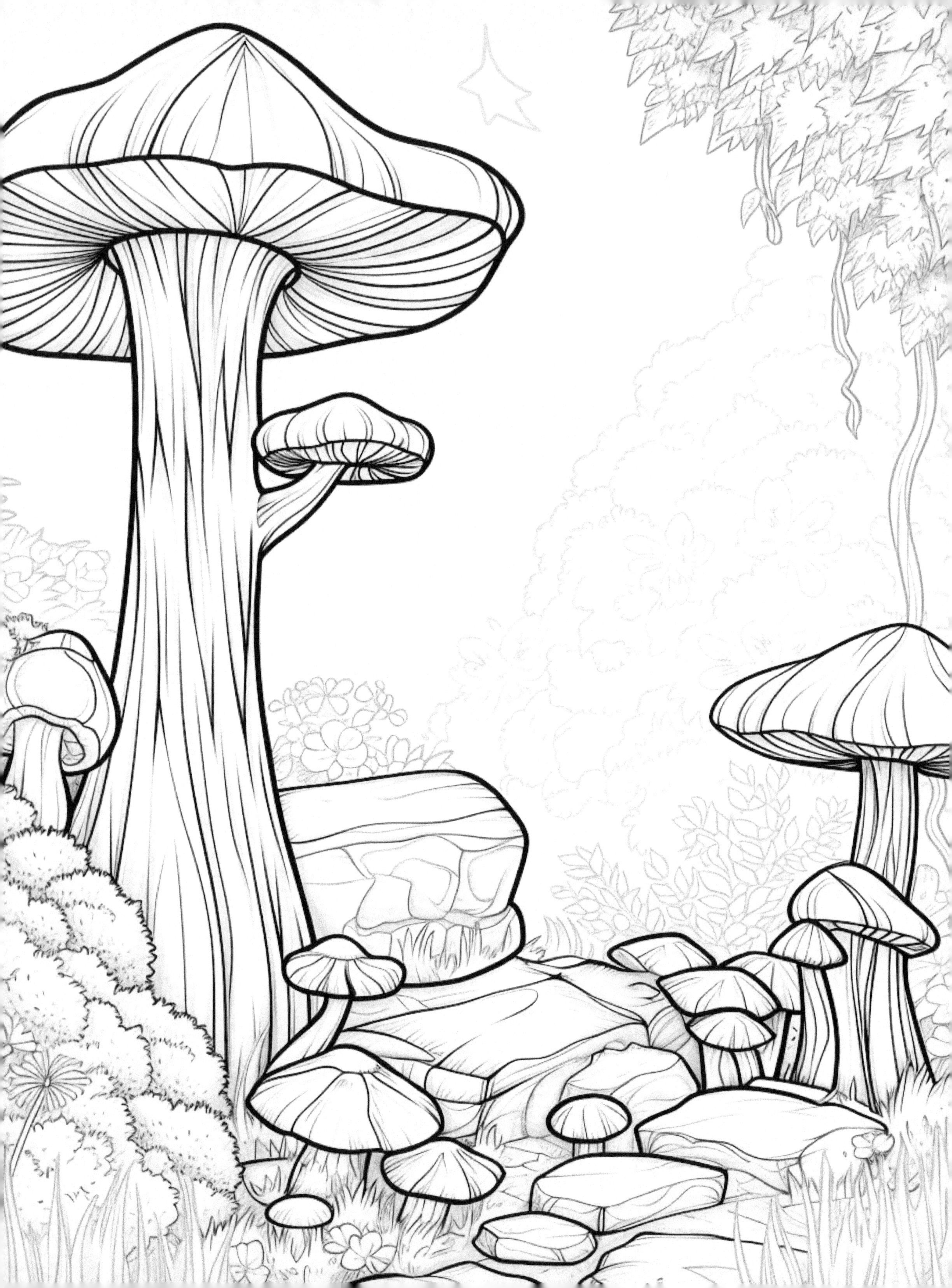

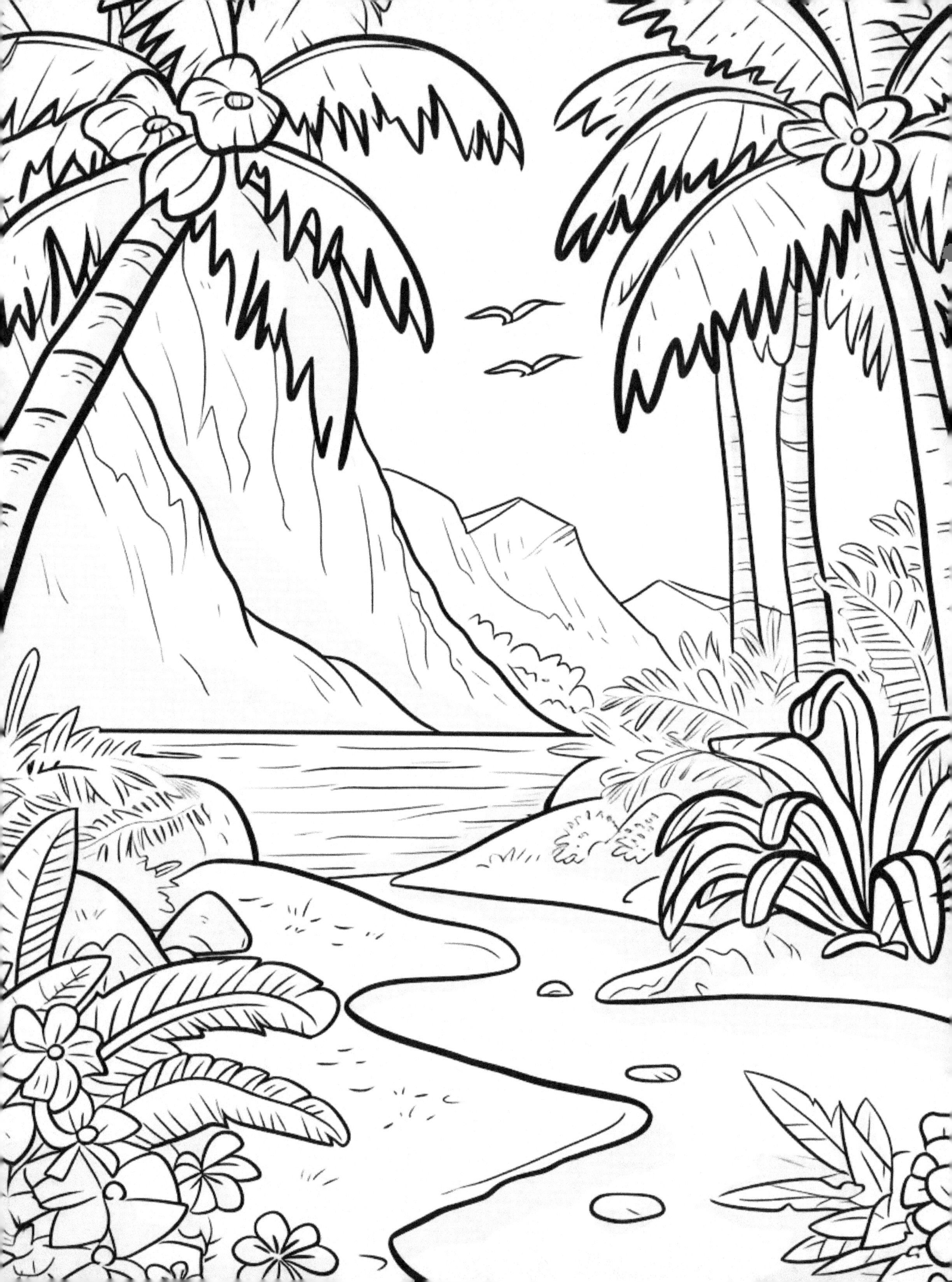

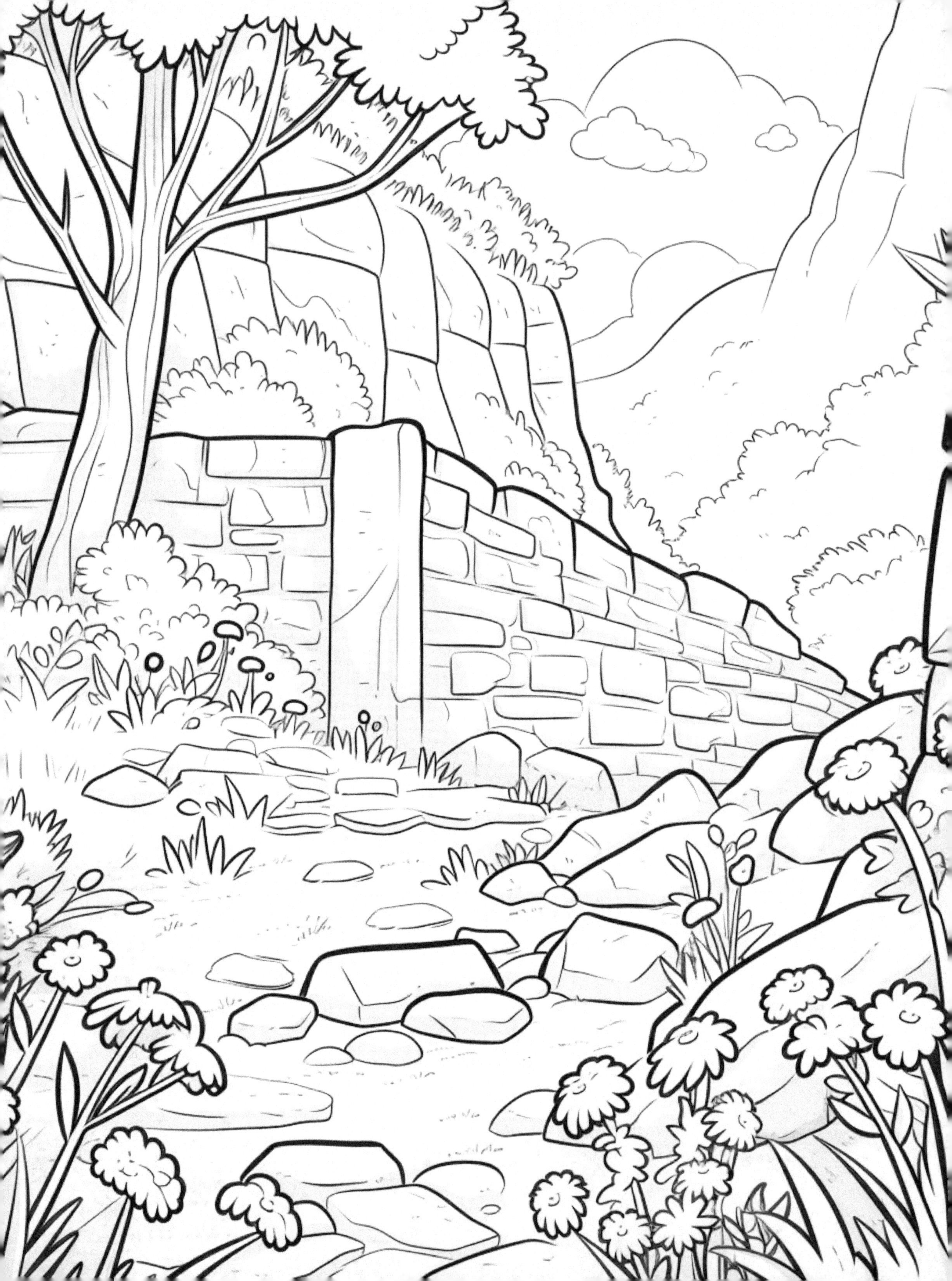

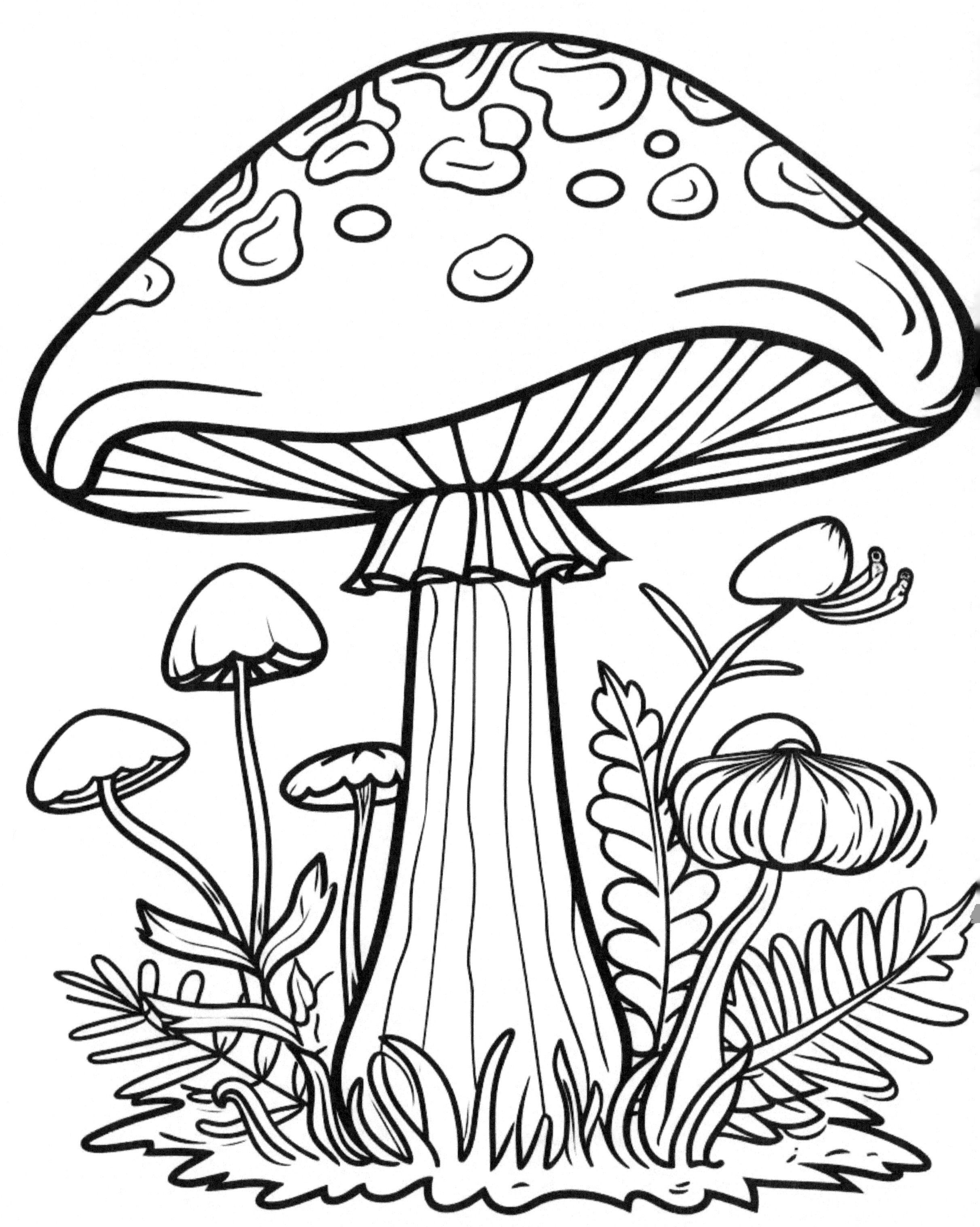

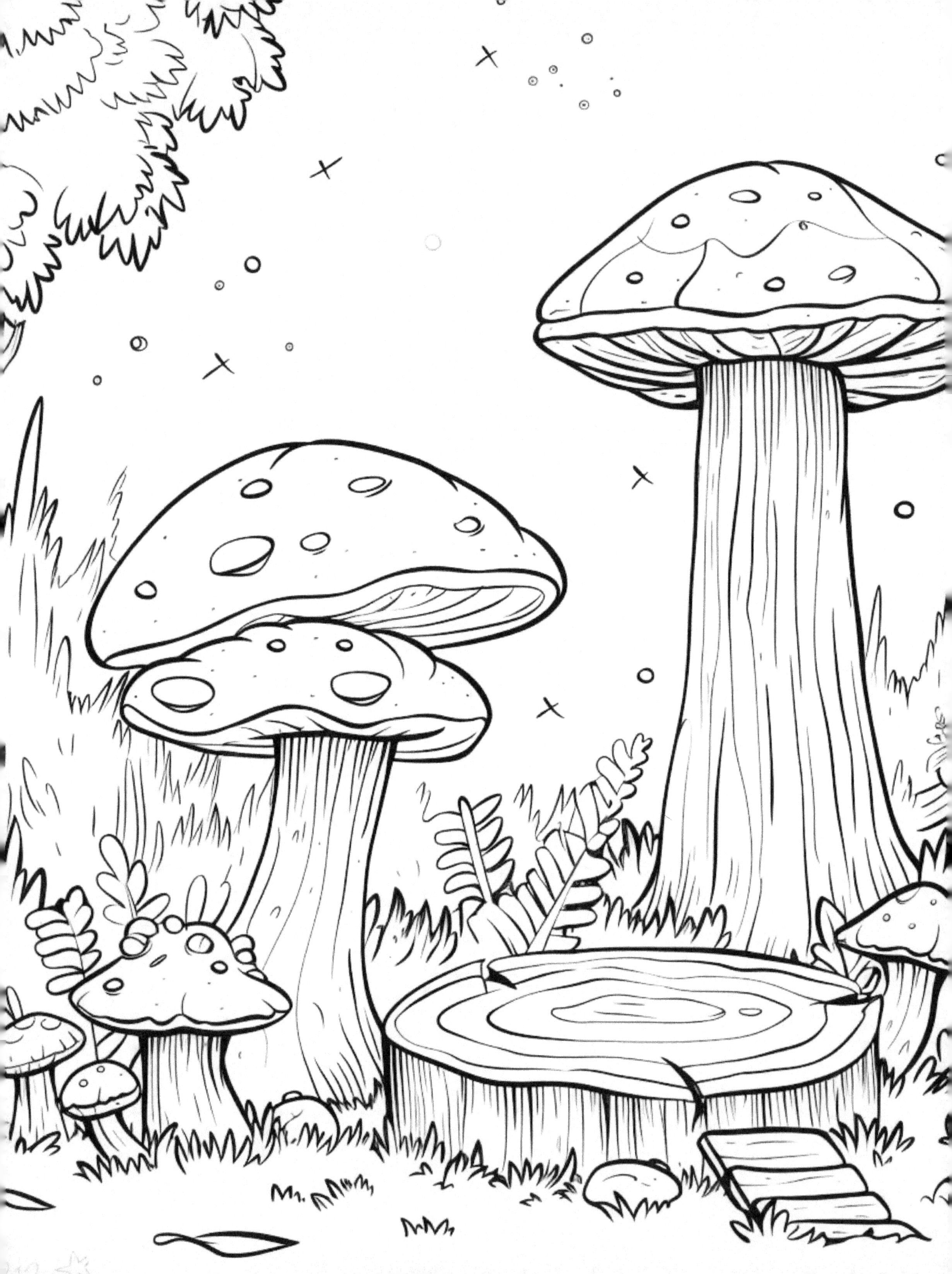

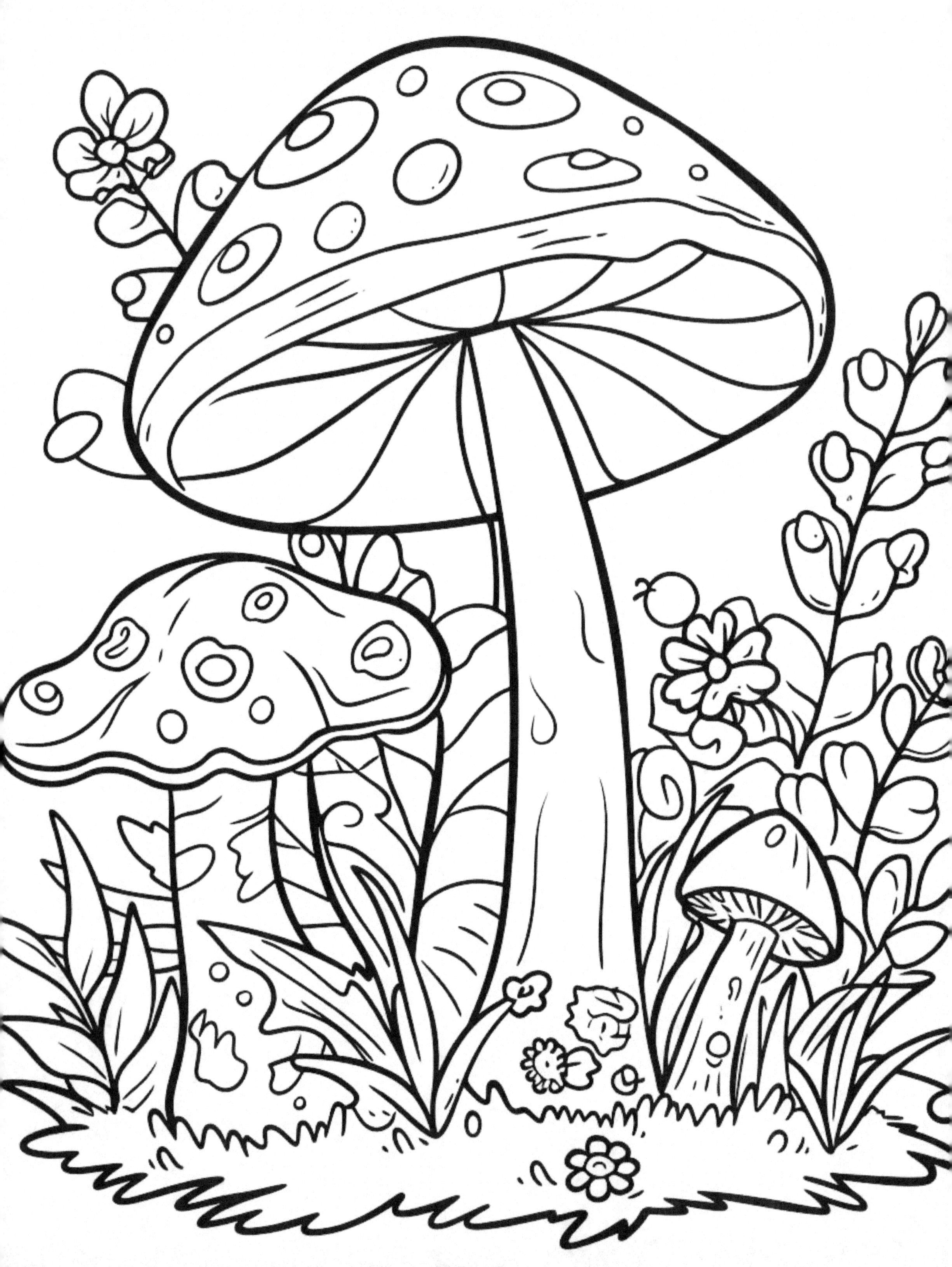

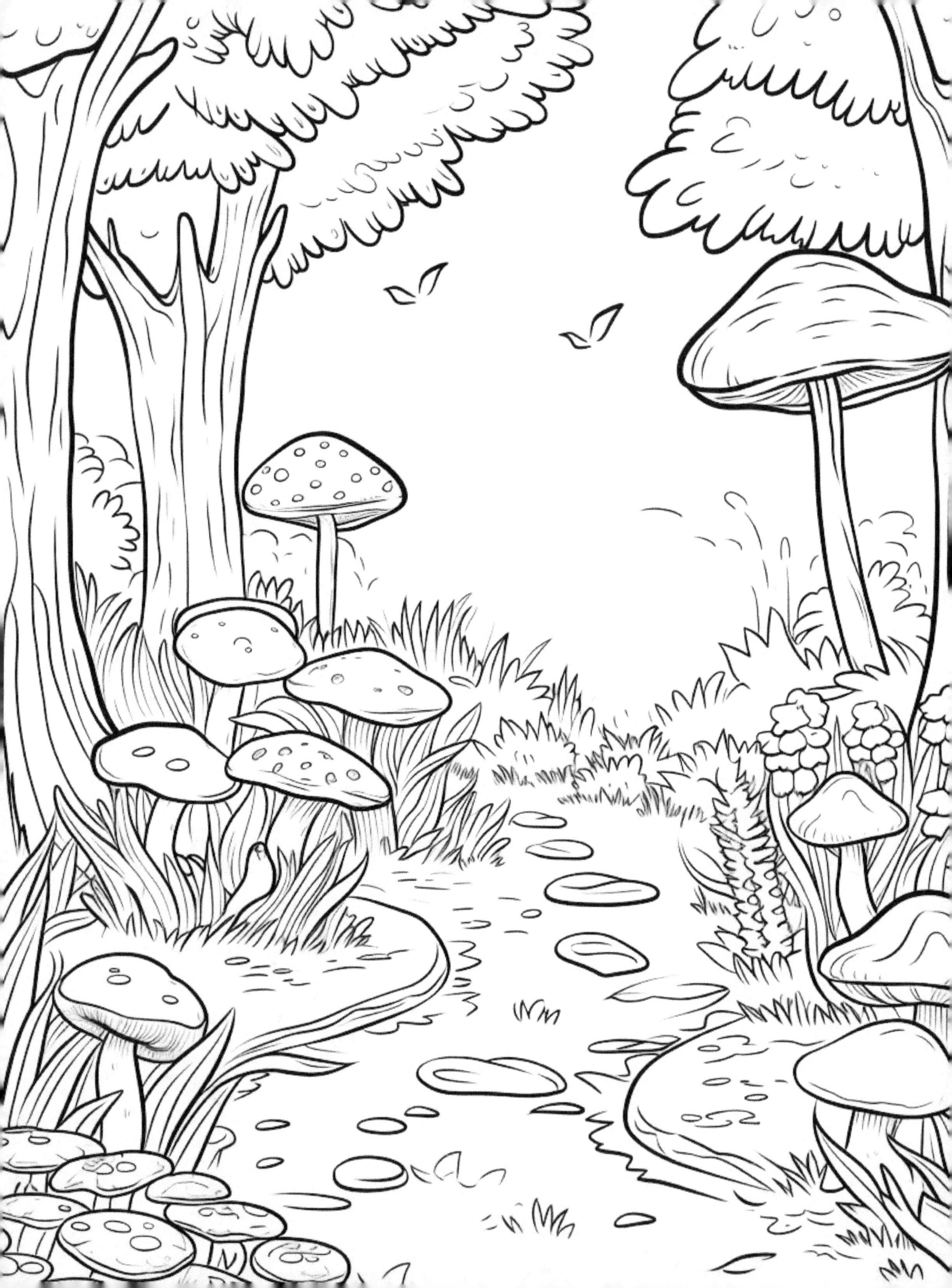

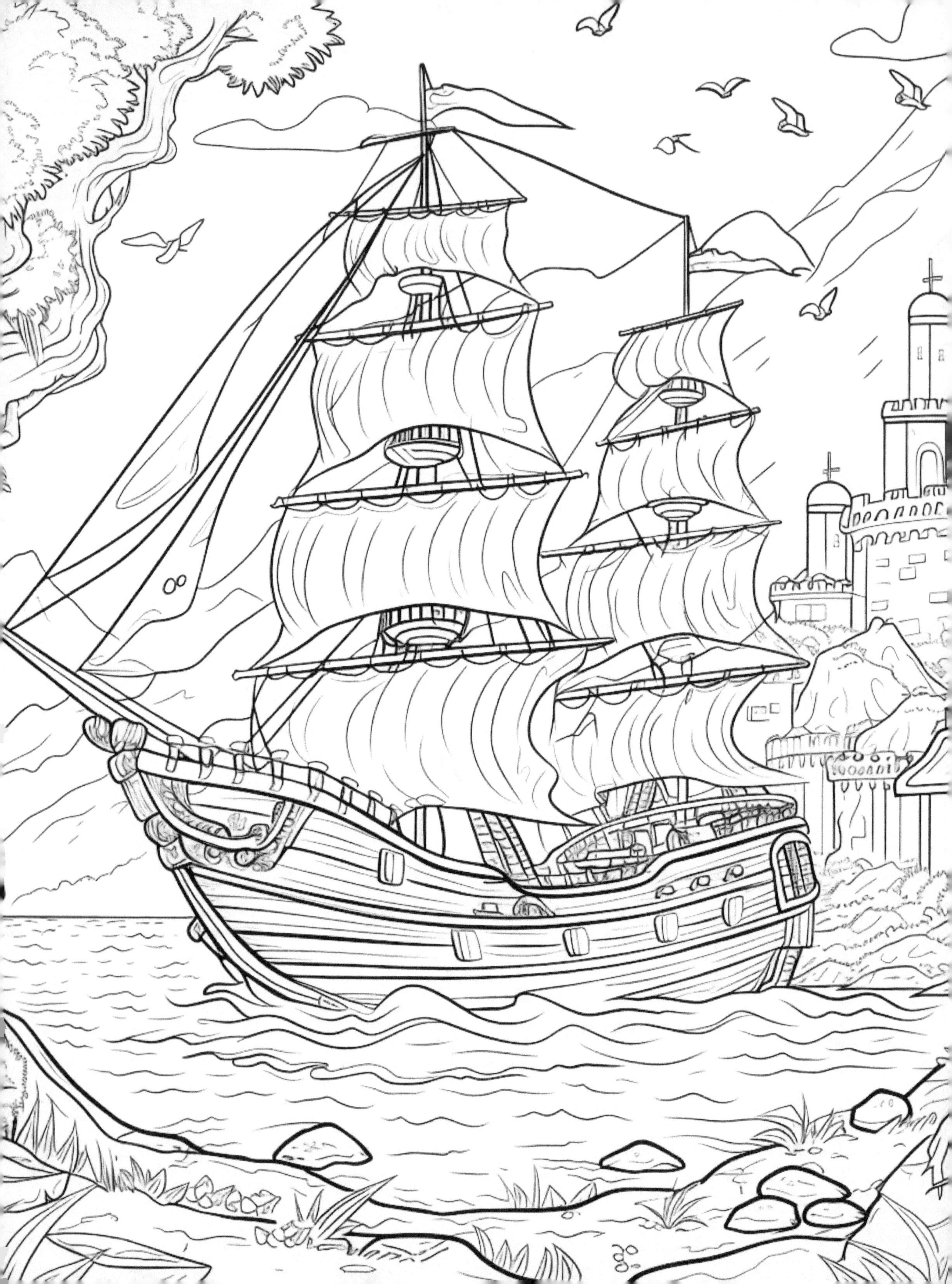

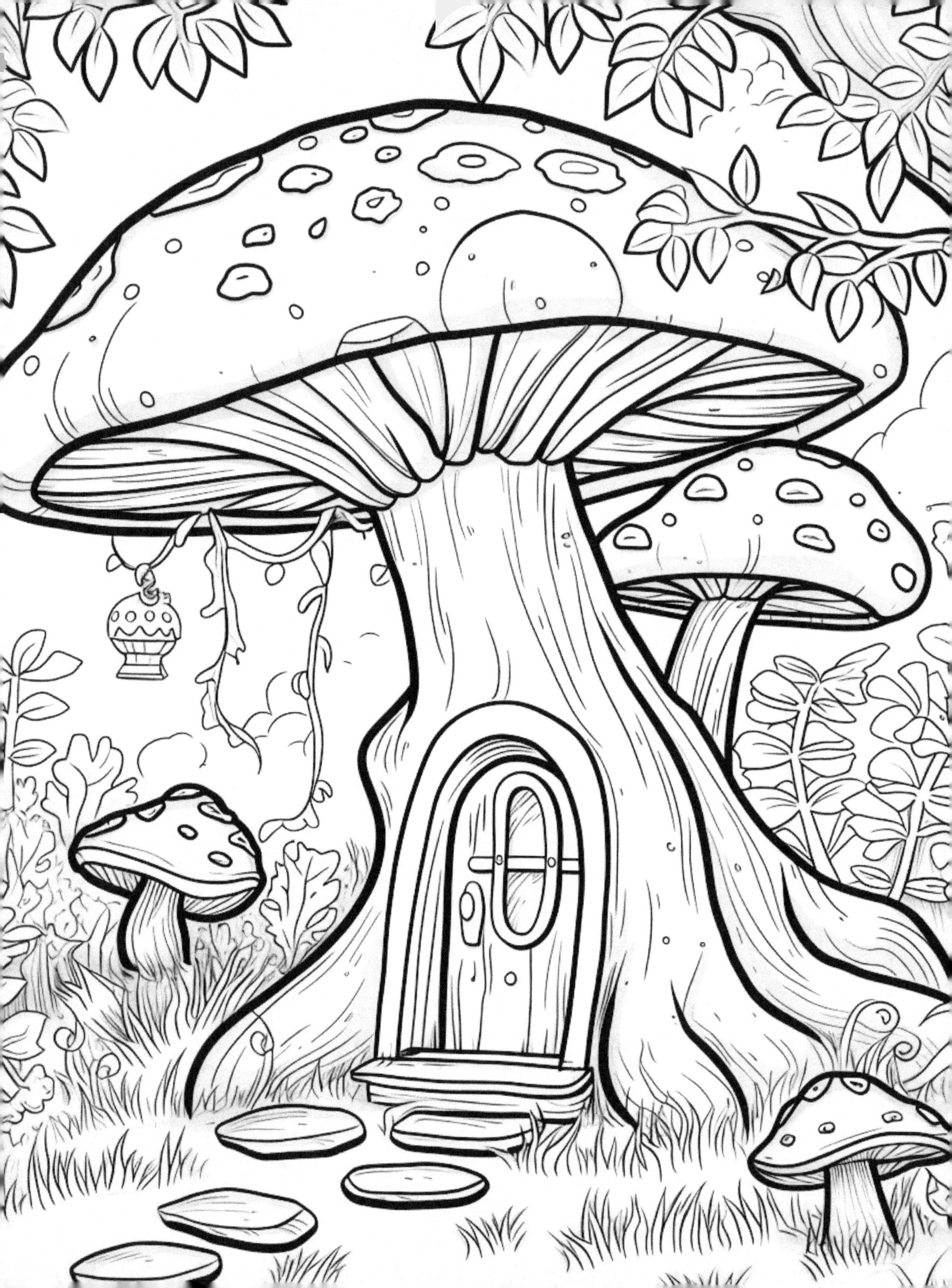

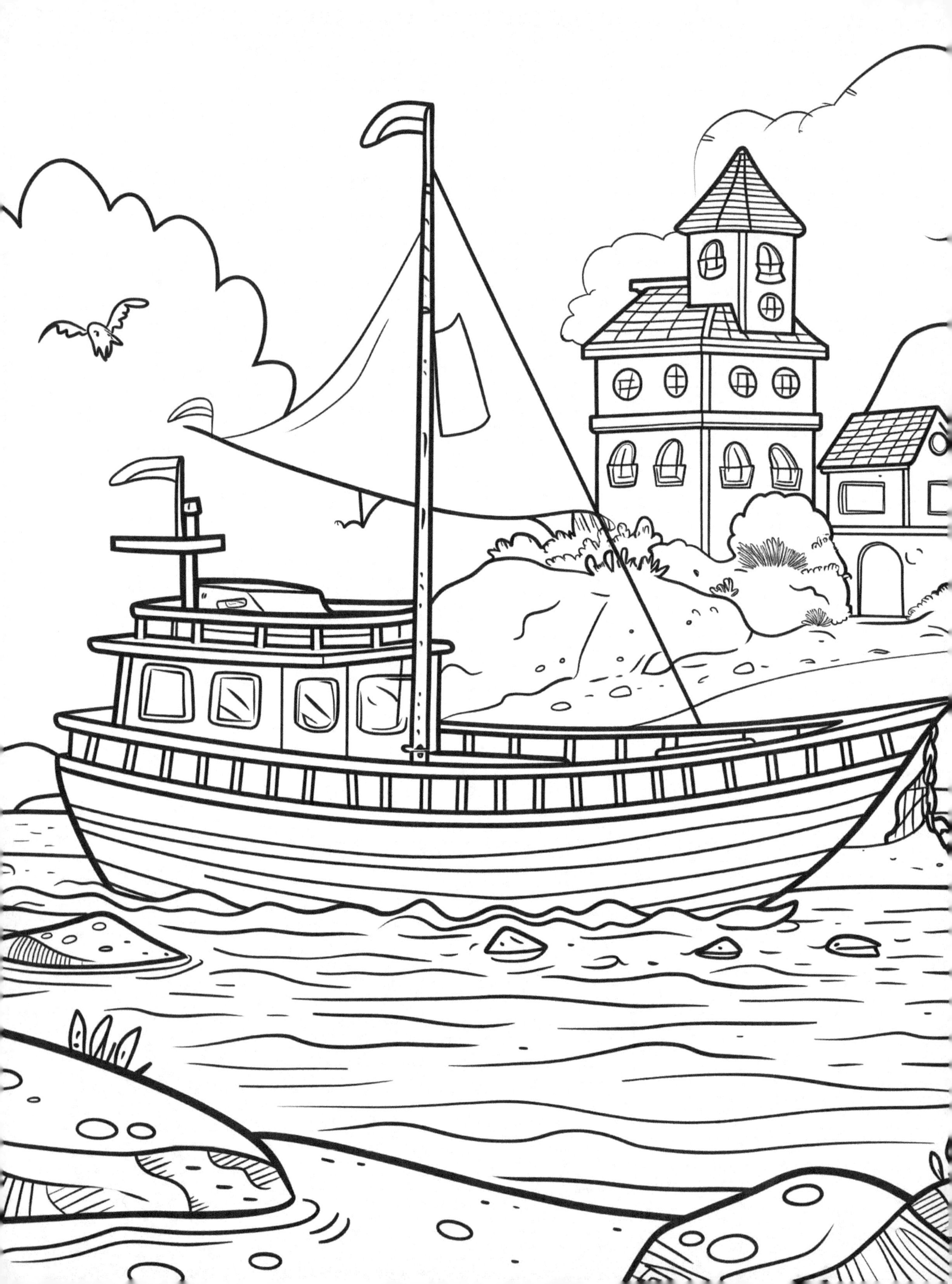

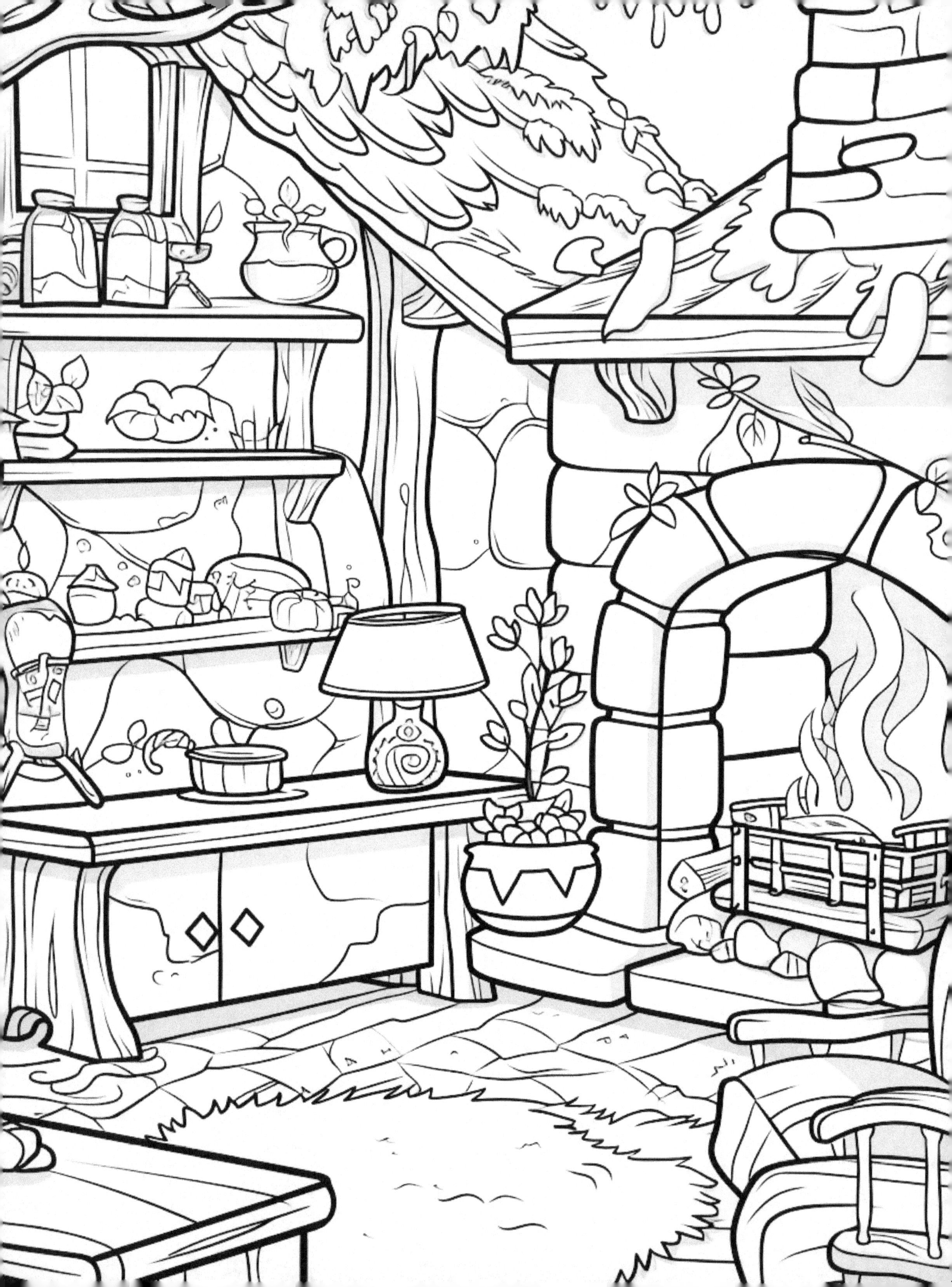

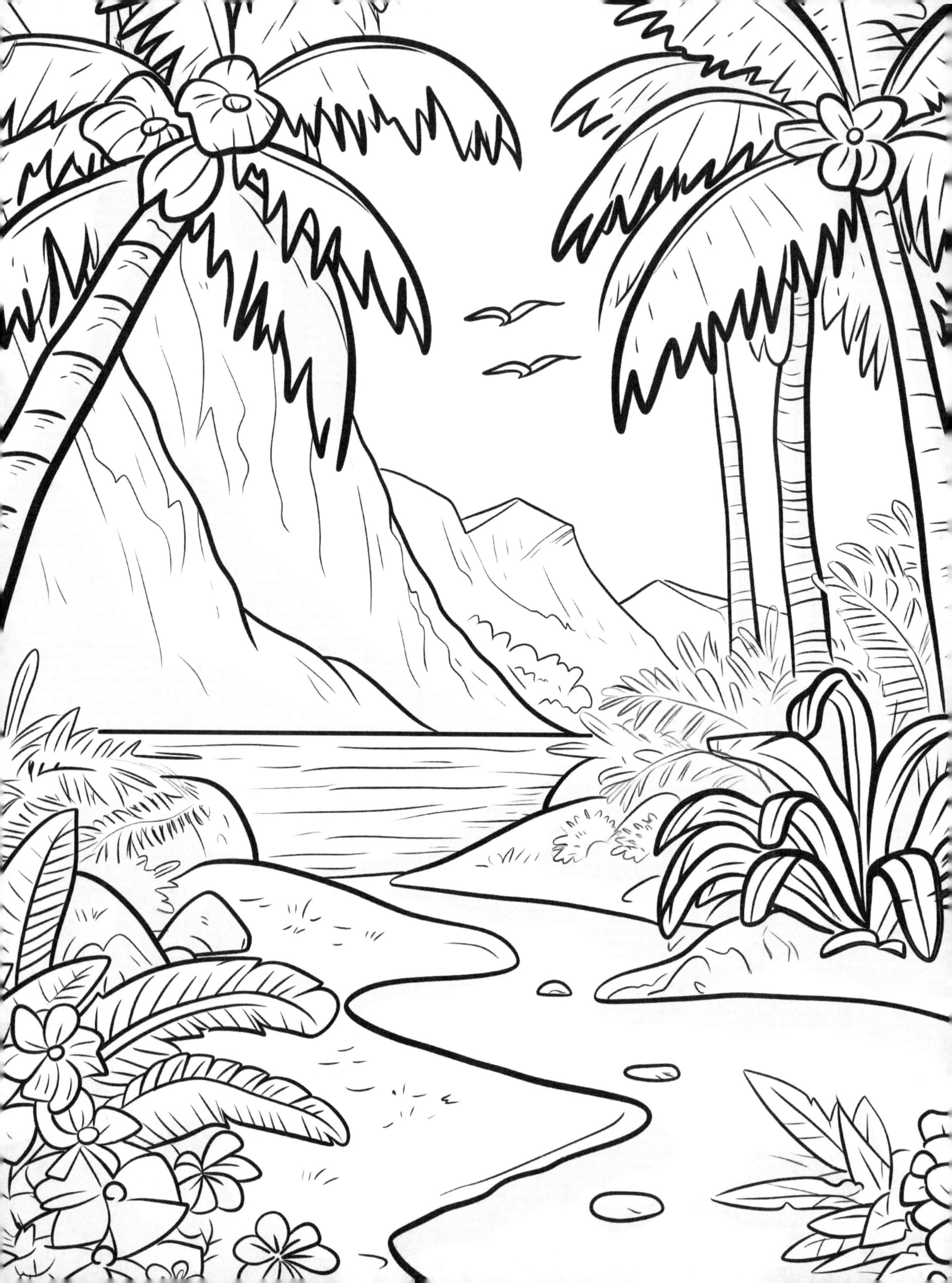

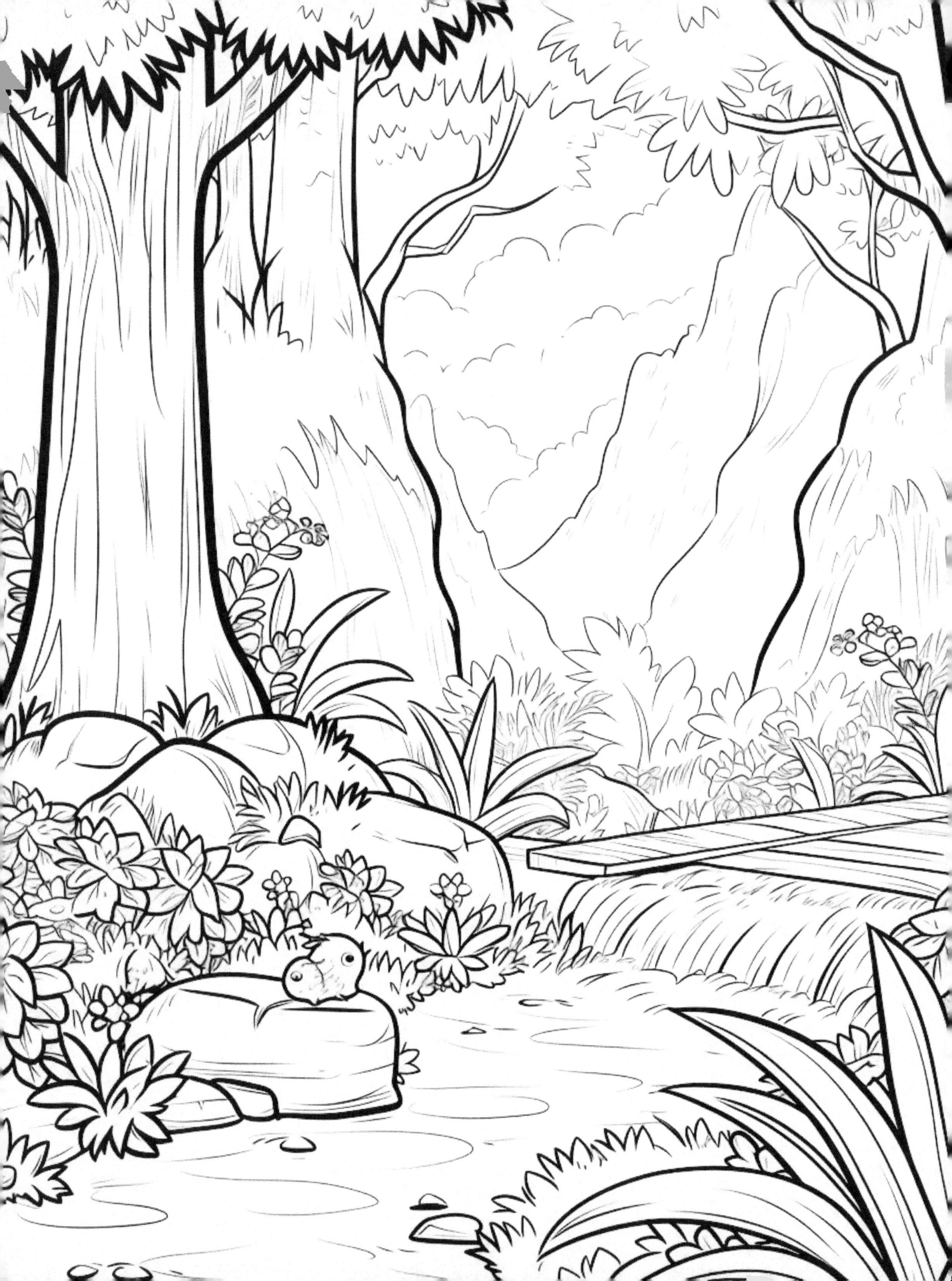

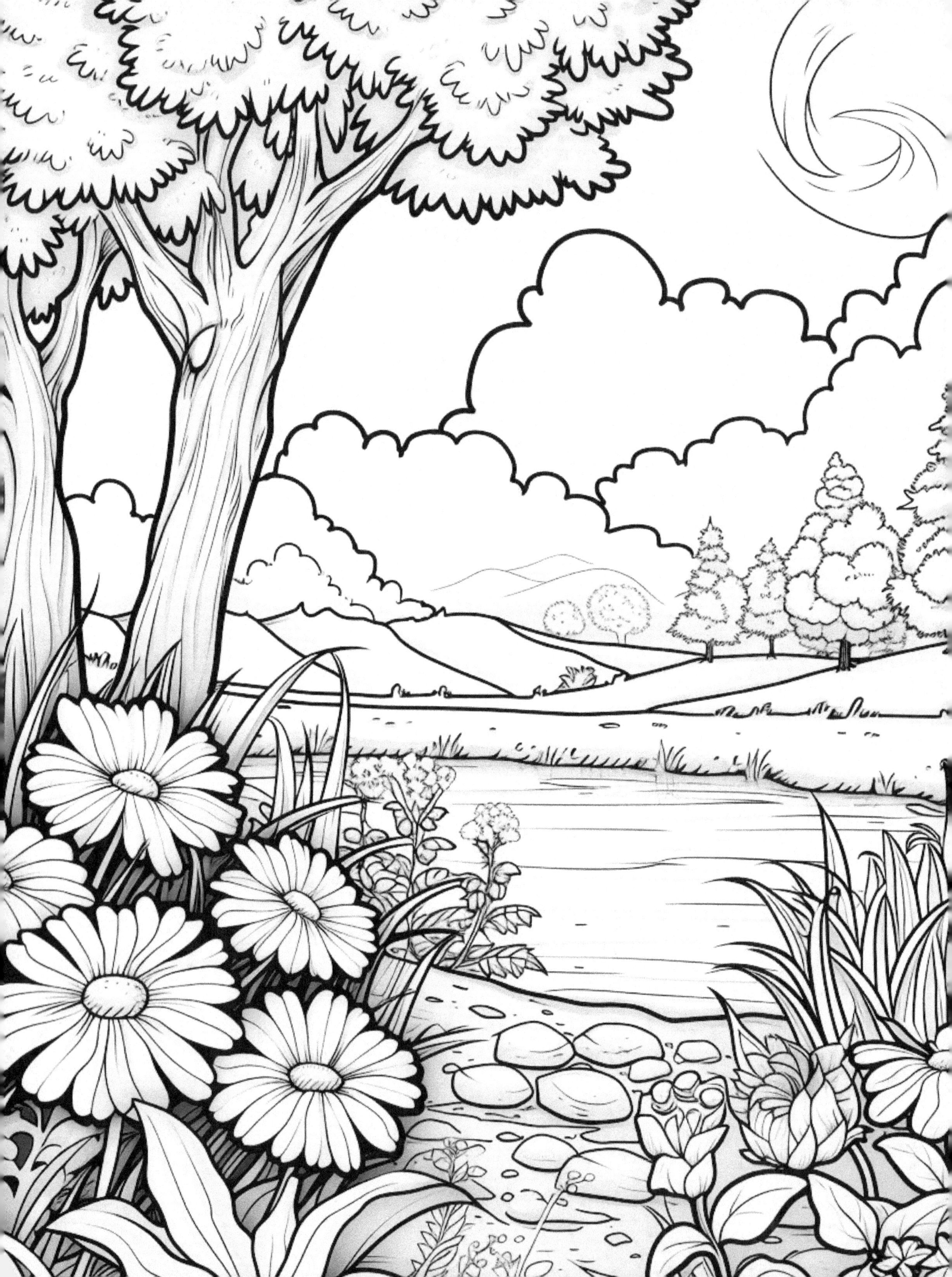

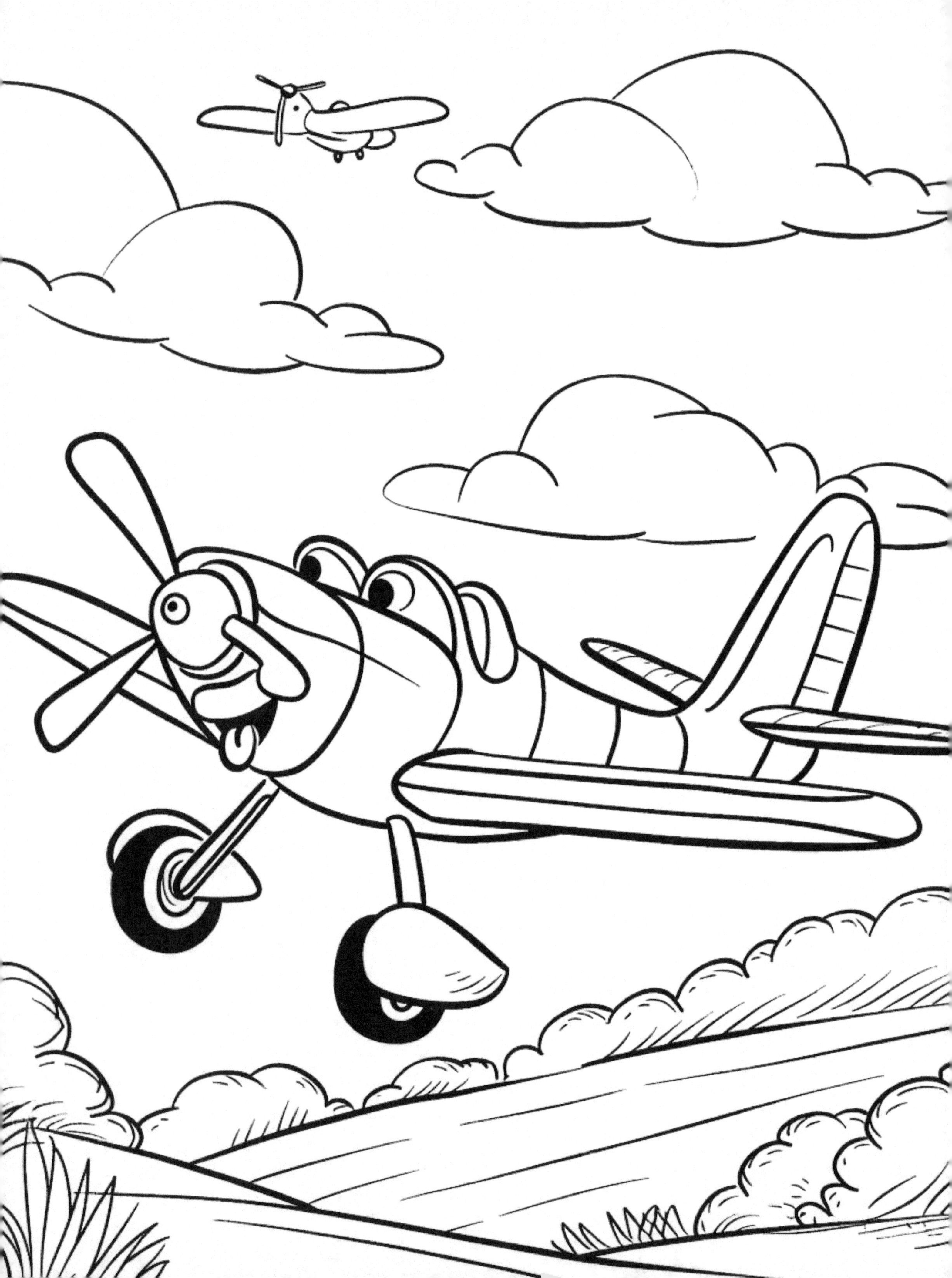

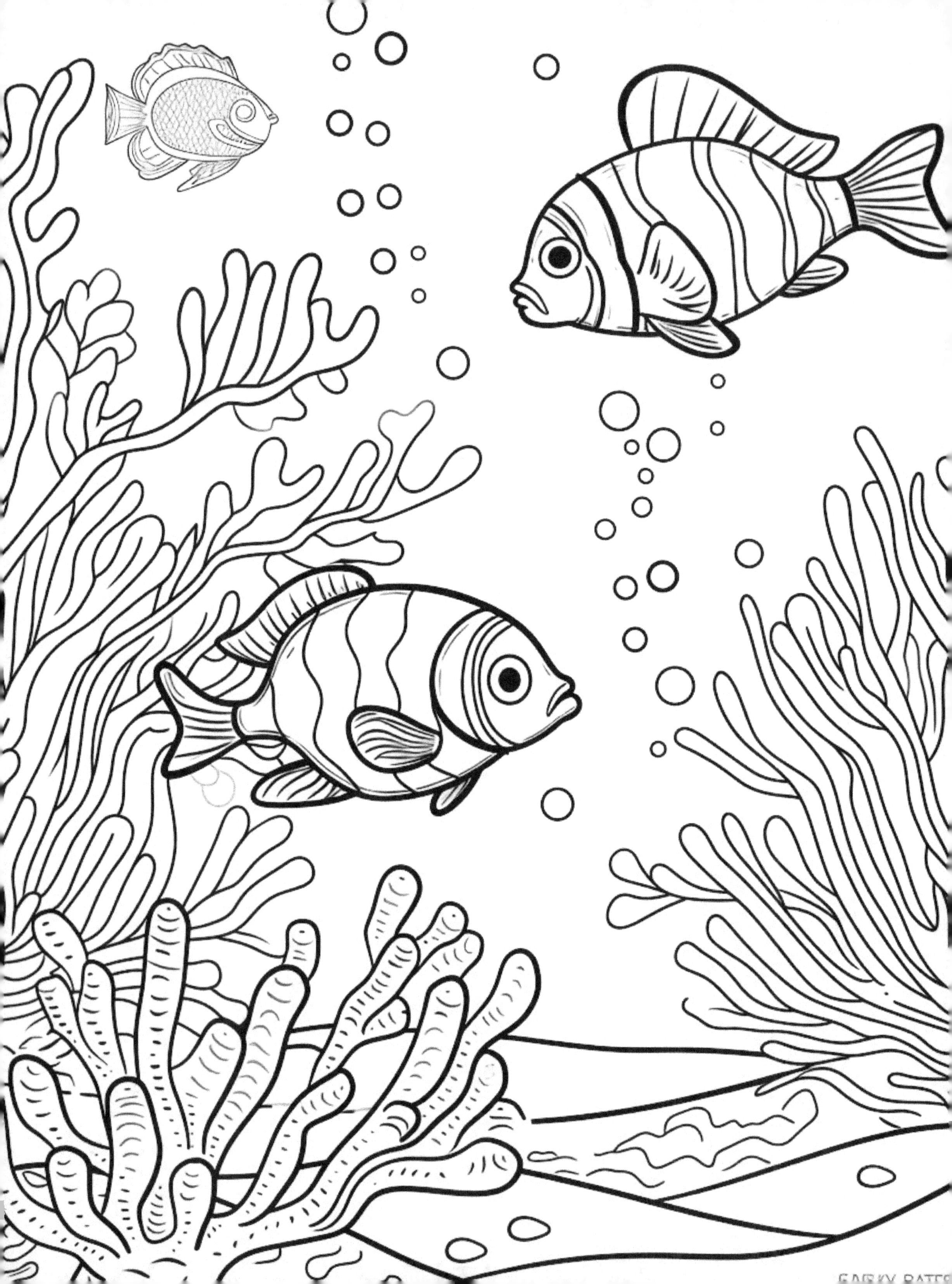

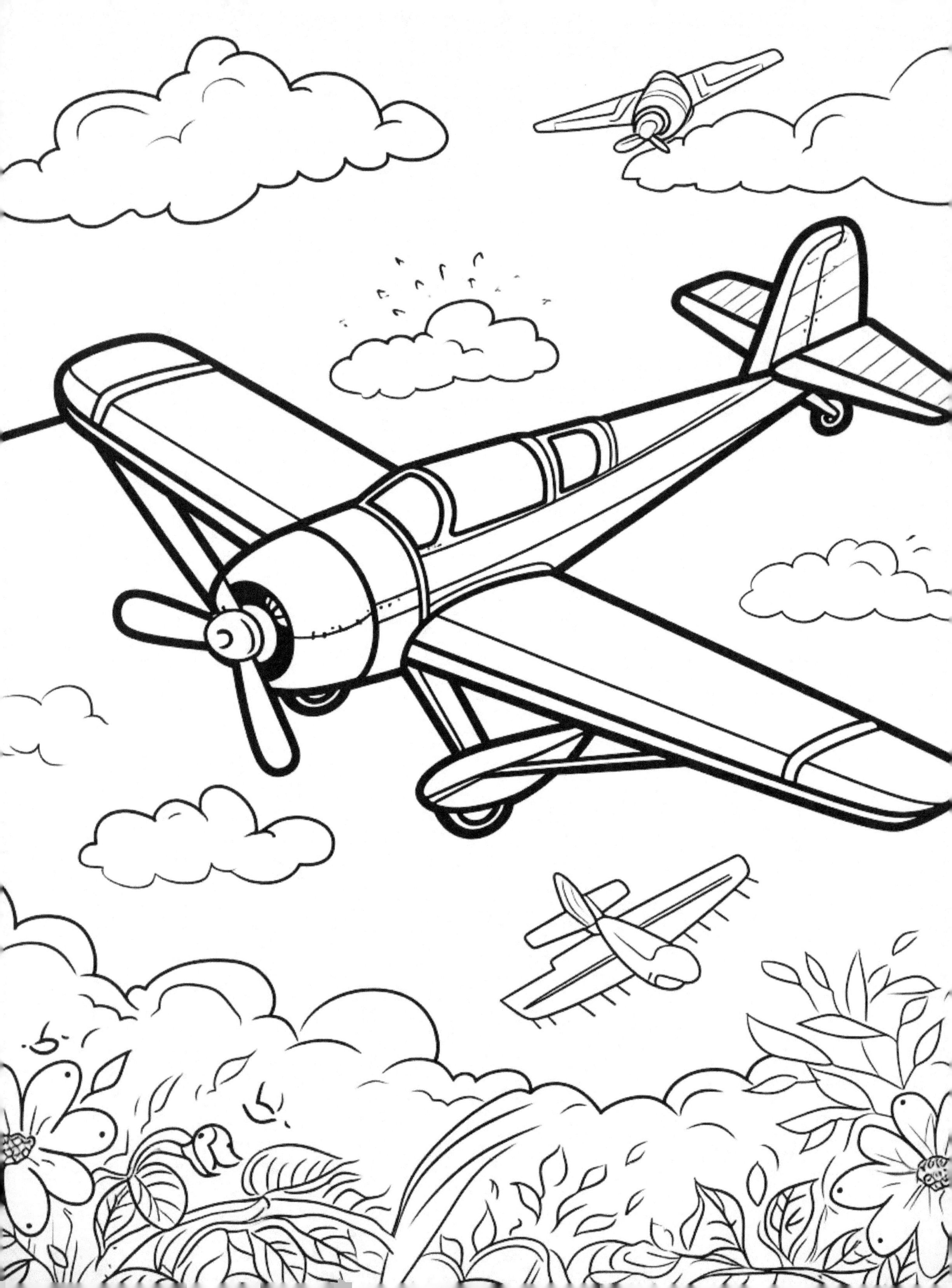

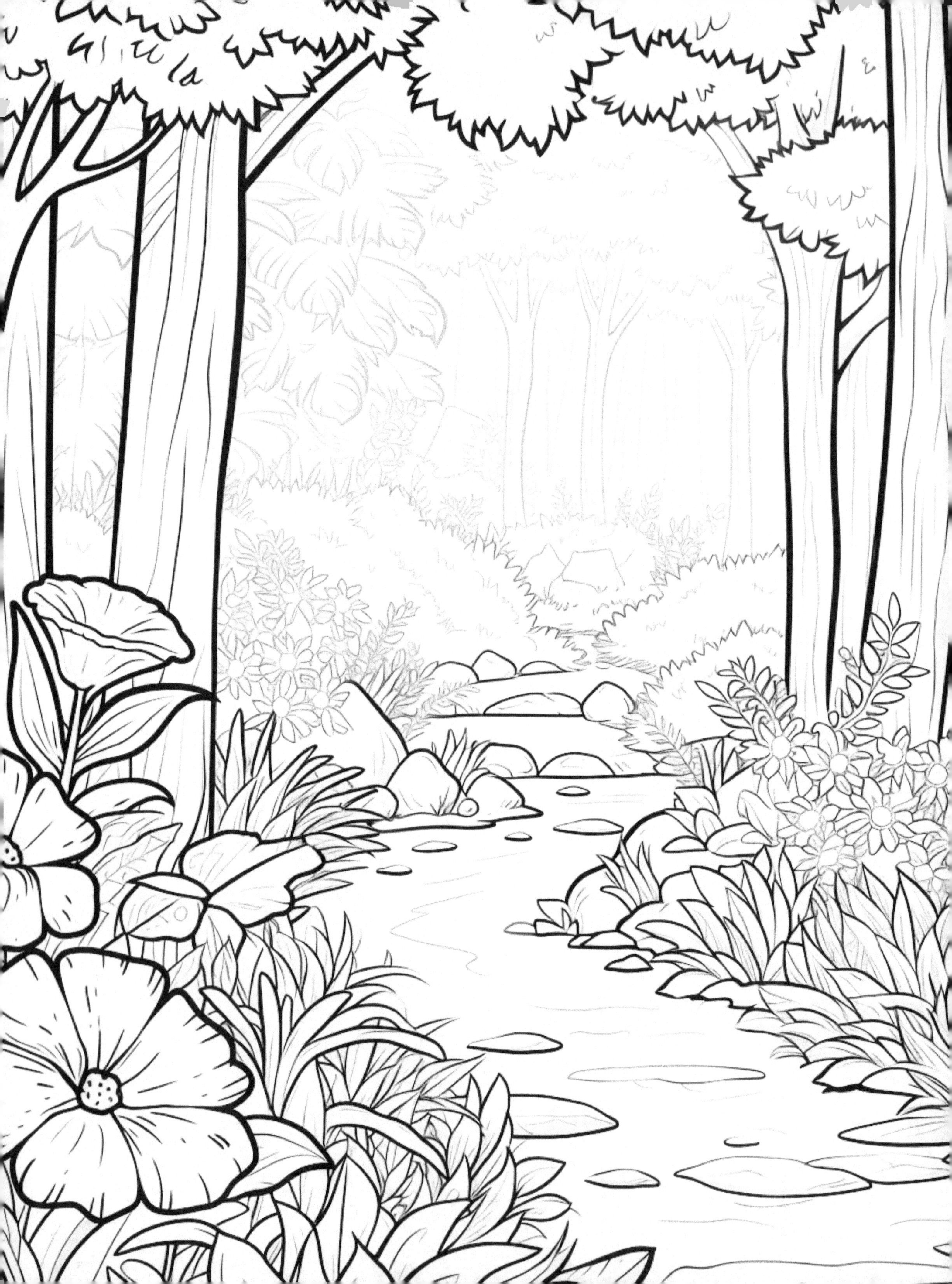

thank you

You've brought these beautiful pages to life with every stroke, creating your own moments of calm and connection.

As you turn the final page, remember that the journey to peace and creativity never ends.

Carry the serenity found here into your everyday life, letting your colors continue to blossom!

Share your artistic journey! I'd love to see your vibrant masterpieces. Leave a review with your picture on Amazon.

**With gratitude for your creative spirit,
Artur Sobolevskij**

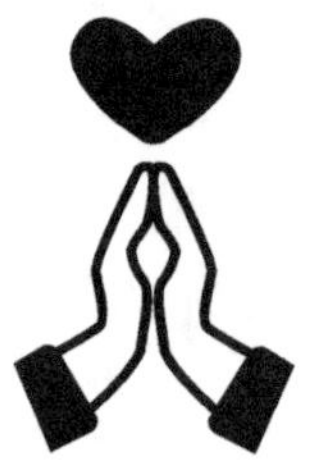

www.ingramcontent.com/pod-product-compliance
Lightning Source LLC
Chambersburg PA
CBHW080025260726
48658CB00007B/2471